T0127718

Adultery Hurts, Stop It!

Ernst Vital

WESTBOW
PRESS®
A DIVISION OF THOMAS NELSON
& ZONDERVAN

WestBow Press books may be ordered through booksellers or by contacting:

WestBow Press
A Division of Thomas Nelson & Zondervan
1663 Liberty Drive
Bloomington, IN 47403
www.westbowpress.com
1 (866) 928-1240

ISBN: 978-1-9736-3443-0 (sc)
ISBN: 978-1-9736-3442-3 (hc)
ISBN: 978-1-9736-3444-7 (e)

Library of Congress Control Number: 2018908449

Print information available on the last page.

WestBow Press rev. date: 7/16/2018

Contents

Introduction vii

Chapter 1   Adultery Hurts 1
Chapter 2   Restoration After Adultery 11
Chapter 3   The Pain of Adultery 15
Chapter 4   How to Repent from Adultery..........................27
Chapter 5   Adultery Costs More Than You Think........................35
Chapter 6   Adultery Destroys Marriages 55
Chapter 7   Satan Attacks Marriages 69
Chapter 8   The Difference Between a Godly Wife and an
               Ungodly Wife 79
Chapter 9   Spiritual Adultery 89

Introduction

I wrote this book, "Adultery Hurts, Stop It" to help victims of infidelity cope with adultery and its aftermath. Discovering that your spouse is cheating on you is one of the worst experiences of your life. When you married the other individual, you literally changed your life completely for them, regardless of whether you are the man or woman. Whereas before, you had certain "privileges" and "freedoms" that came with being single, you agreed to spend the rest of your natural life with your spouse. The two of you made sacred vows before God that were expected to be taken more seriously than any oath taken in a court of law. When you learn your spouse has committed adultery, regardless of how the news comes to you, it is like getting shot in the stomach.

Whereas, moments before, you had thoughts of security that came from the idea of fidelity in the relationship by the two of you, that has now all been ripped away from you. The word cheating is far too mild to describe the level of pain the act brings. Your mind is now a whirlwind of emotions, each vying for dominancy in your thoughts each moment, causing you to feel shocked, angry, depressed, confused, and most of all, being in a state of deep pain.

Your marriage has been hit with infidelity, and you may be wondering what to do or how do you get through this life impacting situation. In this book, you will find some scriptural and practical advice on how to deal with the aftermath of adultery. The first thing you need to do, despite your angry feelings towards your spouse, is to talk to them about the betrayal. This is not going to be an easy conversation, so settle in with your pastor or trusted friend to help get you through. I wrote this book to avoid associating with people involved in sexual immorality. I am referring to abstaining from the sexual immorality that comes from adultery, which is lauded today by this world, and repent from it.

The book of Proverbs provides a detailed outline of the characteristics of the adulterer. He is called simple and senseless and compared to an animal caught in a snare, who is helplessly waiting to be slaughtered. A person who commits adultery has no sense; rather than encountering ill will from an enemy, he or she destroys him or herself. Reading the warnings in this book should be enough to strike fear in anyone's heart and make them crave to change their mind and heart by turning to God and repenting of their sins. This book will teach you how to flee from sexual immorality, then repent from it and live a godly life filled with happiness. Because a lot of people's character is significantly damaged by adultery, the Bible takes many blunt steps to warn and make it clear that adultery contains very serious and terrible consequences.

In this book you will find out how to flee from adultery, lust, learning and sexual immorality. You will also find out what to do in the aftermath of adultery and how to forgive your spouse after they have been unfaithful to you.

When you commit adultery, be aware that in the beginning it only asks for a small down payment, but as time go on, the cost is greater than first thought until the final purchase prices is far greater than you can ever imagine.

Chapter 1

Adultery Hurts

Adultery is the most devastating act against any marriage. If your wife or husband has committed, or is committing adultery, you need to turn yourself toward the Lord and ask for wisdom and courage to help you endure the pain and ask God to give you the ability to hear his voice in the middle of your pain and anger that is screaming out a variety of emotions.

There is no excuse for adultery. The Bible says, "flee youthful lusts" (2 Timothy 2:22). The warning against adultery is also one of the Ten Commandments. "You shall not commit adultery" (Exodus 20:14).

Adultery is the primary temptation that leads to having an affair. This is why the bible does not just want against committing adultery, it admonishes us to avoid the steps that lead to it. The reason for these warnings is the bible lists adultery as one of the only reasons for divorce. This does not mean divorce is God's will for marriage. Rather, the bible always teaches the best course of action is repentance and reconciliation. You should always seek God's direction in prayer along with other wise counsel in this matter before you decide to divorce your spouse.

However, if your wife or husband is defiant about their active adultery and this is not the first time this happened, or they refuse to stop, then you need to be much stronger in your attitude. This is where you may consider separation or possibly a divorce. Staying in a relationship that can expose you to sexually transmitted diseases, as well as great emotional harm, is not God's will for a healthy marriage.

If you decide to move towards divorce, my advice is for you to seek out a Christian counselor to help you through this difficult process.

Seek God's guidance to deal with the aftermath of adultery, for it is much like the stages of grief following a death. It is important to give yourself the right to grieve during this painful moment in your life. Because you have experienced a terrible betrayal, you've been hurt, and those feelings of anger, depression, bitterness and others are perfectly natural. However, you must take these feelings to the Lord in prayer and he will give you peace of mind. Let Him heal your wounded heart. Allow the Lord to wash over you with healing.

If you are the spouse who committed adultery, the most important step you can take is to accept responsibility and admit fault for your actions and the gravity of the pain you've caused. Because of what you have done, you need to have a contrite attitude and recognize the pain and betrayal that you have caused your husband or wife, understanding there is a good chance it will take some time before they express any attitude of forgiveness. It is vital that you be patient. Remember, by your actions, you have sinned against God and against your spouse, committing perjury against the sacred vows you took on your wedding day.

My advice to you is to sincerely repent to God and then your spouse. Please understand, repenting does not mean there will be no consequences for your sins. You must also deal with the results of your actions, some of which may endure for the rest of your life. Rather than make excuses for whatever issues in your marriage may have existed, realize that no matter what circumstances contributed to the breakdown of the relationship that led to you feeling you needed to commit adultery, no one caused you to sin (and that includes the devil). It was your choice.

If you wish to restore your life and repair your marriage, you will have to prove to your spouse that you have truly changed. Many people express sorrow after they have been caught in a particular sin or crime, but often it is sorrow over the consequences rather than godly sorrow over the act itself. The way you can tell the difference is when you are experiencing feelings of sorrow, would you feel that way if no one found out about your sin, or if they did, if there were not consequences. If the answer is no, then your repentance is not sincere. However, if your repentance is sincere, and with patience you understand you must "prove yourself," then there is a good chance your reputation and trust can be regained by your spouse; rather than have a pious attitude of, "well, I said I was wrong and sorry, she needs to forgive me. After all, Jesus said we are to forgive those who wrong us seven times seventy;" acknowledge it is natural for your spouse to be suspicious of you for a while. Trust can be restored, but it only comes as you are open and honest and prove yourself trustworthy.

If you are sincere in wanting your marriage to work, it is not enough to have a sincere heart of repentance. You must also think about a plan to avoid the steps that led to commit adultery in the first place.

The bible says, "A prudent man foreseeth the evil, and hideth himself: but the simple pass on, and are punish" (Proverbs 22:3). In the New Testament, this is further clarified when we are told not just to abstain from evil but from the very appearance of evil. "Abstain from all appearance of evil" (1 Thessalonians 5:22).

This is very practical advice. A common refrain when someone that we did not expect is discovered to have sinned is, "they fell into sin." That is a lie, there is no such thing as falling into sin. The phrase implies that you were just going about life, minding your own business when suddenly, like tripping over a crack in the sidewalk, you stumbled and fell.

Sin is always a conscious act, but before it occurs, sin begins as a thought in the mind. As an example, let's examine the example of the first recorded sin by mankind in Genesis three. Let us start by recording what the actual prohibition God gave Adam and Eve was.

"And the LORD God commanded the man, saying, Of every tree of the garden thou mayest freely eat: But of the tree of the knowledge of good and evil, thou shalt not eat of it: for in the day that thou eatest thereof thou shalt surely die." (Genesis 2:17)

Notice carefully that the prohibition was very specific. Eating of the fruit was wrong, but any other interaction with the tree would not have been sinful. For example, they could pick the fruit from the tree, hold it in their hands and smell it, and they still would not have sinned. I will go a step further and say that based on God's prohibition, by the letter of the law, they could even put the fruit in their mouth and even bite into it, but as long as they didn't swallow any of it, they would not have "eaten" any of it, and thus would not have sinned.

Now, after the serpent tempted Eve, notice what happened before she ate the fruit

"And when the woman saw that the tree was good for food, and that it was pleasant to the eyes, and a tree to be desired to make one wise, she took of the fruit thereof, and did eat, and gave also unto her husband with her; and he did eat. (Genesis 3:6)

There were a few steps involved in Eve partaking of the fruit. First, she looked. She saw it was good for food. Then she noticed the fruit was pleasant to look at, in other words it was enticing. Then she wanted to become wise and thought this fruit would meet this need. Only then did she reach out and take the fruit and eat it.

Now let's examine this event in light of the previous mentioned scriptures about seeing the evil and hiding yourself and abstaining from all appearance of evil.

Remember, we showed that taking the fruit and holding it up to her mouth was not wrong, but if you were there that day, would you have advised her to do so. Likewise, when she placed it in her mouth, she had not sinned yet, but she was dangerously close. Would you have said, "that's okay Eve, enjoy the sensation of the taste in your mouth but just make sure you don't swallow any of the juices or the fruit. Spit it out right before then." Of course you wouldn't, at least not if you have even half a brain.

We now have the hindsight of 6,000 years of human history to see what the horrifying consequences of Adam and Eve's sin has wrought. We also have the benefit of having a complete bible that warns us of these consequences, as well as giving instruction for us on how to keep from sinning, and this includes the sin of adultery.

With this knowledge, if I had been there in the garden of Eden, long before Eve was tempted, I would have advised Adam to dig a moat around the tree. Then I would have had him stock it with crocodiles and alligators to prevent someone from swimming across. I would have also advised him to place a wall with barbed wire around the tree, then booby-trap the entire area with landmines. I would tell Adam it would be better for one of his sons or daughters to die trying to get to the tree then for the entire human race to be damned. Would you not agree that this is good advice?

If so, then the same logic would apply in principle to every sin, namely that the way to avoid sin is not just to not do it, but to take prudent steps to avoid the things that place you on the pathway to committing sin. Eve did not sin until she actually ate of the fruit, but if she had not been on the pathway by taking, holding, then putting the fruit in her mouth, she would never have arrived at the destination of sin.

The attitude a Christian should have is not to find out exactly what is wrong so you can see how close you can get to sin, but to find out what is sin so you can stay as far away from it as you can.

There is a story about a king who lived during biblical times who was wanting to hire a new man to drive his chariot. Being the king, he wanted the best charioteer for this important position. Over the next several weeks his advisors gathered the best drivers in the land who went through a battery of tests including background checks and tests to ensure the highest standards of loyalty no matter what, along with various tests of skills and ability.

Finally, after weeding out most of the hundreds of candidates, he was left with four men who had passed every qualification to this point. One of these men would receive the highly coveted position of Royal Charioteer. The king had one final "test" to decide who would be the one he wanted. He would ask them each a single question.

"If you were driving me in my royal chariot on a narrow mountain road with a high mountain on one side and a sheer drop off of several hundred feet on the other side and you had to get me to my destination in a hurry, how close could you safely get my chariot to the edge of the road?"

The first one proudly proclaimed, "Your majesty, I can keep your horses going in a straight line, never wavering while following the contours of the road. Because of my skill, I can keep the chariot wheel less than an inch from the edge of the drop-off, never varying more than a hair's breadth."

Dismissing him, the king brought in the second man and asked the same question. "Sir, I am an expert in not just driving the chariot, but I can 'feel' every motion it makes. I can drive the horses furiously while keeping the wheel right on the edge of the drop off but never letting any part of the chariot cross over. I can ensure your safety with every turn of the wheel."

Thanking him, the king sent him out and brought in the third man. This candidate was even more confident. "Your royal highness, I have years of experience driving other nobles, and I know the importance of ensuring your orders are followed while also making sure you arrive safely as quickly as possible. I can not only drive the chariot closer to the drop off than any other man alive, I can even have the majority of the wheel hanging off the edge with just a small portion remaining on the road, all while maintaining complete control over the chariot, never once putting you in any danger."

Finally, the last man came in. The king was curious what this man would say since every man had been more daring then the previous one regarding the risks they were willing to take to prove their ability. He asked the man the same question he asked the previous three men.

"My king, I have no idea how close I could come to the edge. I am sorry if this answer disappoints you and if it means I do not get the job I completely understand. The reason I do not know the answer is because I would never attempt anything so foolish. I realize the importance of being the charioteer for his royal majesty and how important you are to the kingdom. If we were driving on such a road, I would take care to keep your chariot as far from the edge as I could. I would instead attempt to have the other wheel rubbing up against the rock on the mountain side of the road. In this way I would be doing my utmost to make your safety of paramount importance."

The king was very pleased with this man's answer, for he knew this person understood the importance of not taking foolish chances. This was precisely the quality and skill he was looking for.

The same should be true for God's people when it comes to sin. Rather than trying to see how close we can get to the fire without being burned, we should instead try to find out where the boundary is and then stay as far away from it as we can.

At the de-militarized zone, or DMZ in Korea there is a building where both sides meet for negotiations and meetings. In the room is a table with a line across it from one end to the other and extending across the middle of the room. This line is the border between North and South Korea. Interestingly, you can cross the line on one side of the table with no ramifications. However, if you cross on the other side of the table, no matter how briefly or small the distance, you have officially defected to North Korea and cannot return to the other side.

I am not going to go into the details of how horrible life is in North Korea, especially for Christians except to say this. In the political prison camps conditions are so horrible there have been times when women have resorted to eating their own children.

Think about how foolish it would be for a person to play around and tell someone, "watch how close I can get to the border without crossing as they have their shoe right on the edge of the line. That would not be a good idea because all it would take would be a single misstep or someone jokingly pushing you or bumping into you. In an instant you are now prevented from coming back, all because you wanted to play around, living on the edge.

The same thing is true with sin. Don't just avoid it, when the bible says, "a prudent man foreseeth the evil, and hideth himself," this is what it is talking about. A wise man takes steps to keep himself as far from the edge of the cliff or the border as possible. This way if you stumble and make a misstep you are still safely on the right side of the line.

When it comes to avoiding adultery, especially if you have already stumbled and committed this sin and are attempting to salvage your marriage, it is vital that you follow this advice. Regardless of how sincere you are that you are never going to allow this to happen again, do not deceive yourself about the relationship. If you choose to see other person, even if just one last time to end it or "remain friends," be advised you are setting yourself up for failure. I am not saying that it is an absolute certainty you will stumble into adultery again, but I will say it is highly probable because you are getting too close to the border. Decide to take steps to ensure you are not going to put yourself in any type of compromising position. If you have to meet with them to break it off, take someone you trust with you, or even better yet, do it via a phone call, email or text, while including having someone trusted in on the conversation to ensure you have a witness as well as be able to jump in to help you if things get dicey.

You should also take a self-diagnostic and ask what situations or areas are prone to cause you think adulterous thoughts. For instance, does watching women in mini-skirts or bikinis cause you to become aroused. For women, is it seeing handsome men with their shirt off in sexually suggestive poses? Whatever it is, stay away from the border and avoid those situations.

This may mean having to separate yourself from some of your closest friends. They may not by themselves be a temptation, but if they like to take you to visit places that lead you to temptations, or their conversations produce unclean thoughts, then you need to politely stop seeing them. Do not have a close friendship with someone who is adulterous or sympathetic towards adultery. This is what the Scriptures say for healing your heart.

"Wherein ye greatly rejoice, though now for a season, if need be, ye are in heaviness through manifold temptations: That the trial of your faith, being much more precious than of gold that perisheth, though it be tried with fire, might be found unto praise and honour and glory at the appearing of Jesus Christ: Whom having not seen, ye love; in whom, though now ye see him not, yet believing, ye rejoice with joy unspeakable and full of glory: Receiving the end of your faith, even the salvation of your souls." (1 Peter 1:6-9)

In Isaiah 59:1 it says, "Behold, the LORD'S hand is not shortened, that it cannot save; neither his ear heavy, that it cannot hear." You are the key to protecting your marriage. Stop adultery.

Chapter 2

Restoration After Adultery

You walk in darkness, stumbling and unable to see what you stumble over. Why? Because you are caught in sexual sin. Because of your foolish indiscretions, you are now experiencing a disconnect from God. Adultery can move you from a lavish lifestyle to the courtroom; from life to death. How sad that sexual appetites can seem so pleasurable in the beginning but instead they are like a ravenous beast that often devours your own soul and flesh.

Rather than many religious leaders who attempt to scare people away from sin by claiming that it is not desirable, the bible tells the unvarnished truth about sin, warning against it while also acknowledging that in the beginning it is a pleasant experience.

"Stolen waters are sweet, and bread eaten in secret is pleasant. But he knoweth not that the dead are there; and that her guests are in the depths of hell." (Proverbs 9:17-18)

Speaking of Moses, it says, "Choosing rather to suffer affliction with the people of God, than to enjoy the pleasures of sin for a season" (Hebrews 11:25).

Adultery hardens the heart towards a husband and wife. Where once both were deeply in love, they are now bitter enemies. Adultery is a selfish act committed against the sacred institution of marriage. God can help you overcome the damage you have done if there is sincere repentance. Adultery's goal is to destroy the marriage.

"But whoso committeth adultery with a woman lacketh understanding: he that doeth it destroyeth his own soul. A wound and dishonour shall he get; and his reproach shall not be wiped away. For jealousy is the rage of a man: therefore he will not spare in the day of vengeance." (Proverbs 6:32-34)

Often, the only way out of adultery's destructive relationship is to repent and do what is right, regardless of your prideful feelings. Adultery is a painful situation. When brought into the open it will make you bitter or better. It depends on the choice that you make. God can restore you, if you are willing to admit you are wrong. True repentance is unconditional and takes full responsibility for your wrongdoing. A truly repentant person is always desperate to be forgiven for what he or she has done rather than over concerns for the penalty or placing blame or responsibility on other people.

Adultery causes a breakdown in the sacred bond of trust entered into when the marriage vows are taken, causing a spirit of separation, making reconciliation nearly impossible. The type of love God called you to have is one where you forgive and love your enemies. Sexual sin hardens the heart and closes it off to forgiveness. I will be the first to admit forgiveness is not easy, but God says you have to forgive others.

I am not downplaying the seriousness of adultery or the hurt you are entitled to feel; I want to say in complete love and kindness and empathy that what you are experiencing pales in comparison to the wrongs done to others throughout history. A reading of the accounts of the martyrs will reveal how they have had to endure betrayals far more severe. This betrayal involves torture and loss of life even unto this day. Of course, we will not mention the ultimate betrayal where

Jesus Christ, the Creator of all things, including us, was betrayed by his own creation and sentenced to the most humiliating form of death possible.

When you are caught in sexual sin you are in darkness and cannot see the danger right in front of you. Adultery provides a great deception, causing Christians to lose their spiritual vision that enables them to see what is right or wrong. This blindness can become so severe that it causes some Christians to believe that God is willing to turn away his eyes from the sin of adultery in extenuating circumstances, providing them with an excuse to continue their adulterous life. I often wonder how many marriages broken by adultery are never restored simply because of pride and disobedience. The offender ends up being more concerned about the feelings of their friends and parents rather than the feelings of their husband or wife.

A genuine repentance results in a sincere turning to God, followed by a confession of sin with a sincere commitment never to commit the offense again. Nearly everyone is sorry about their adultery when caught, but because the motivation is not on sorrow for the sin itself, they never obtain victory over this sin. Being sorry is not enough, you need a genuine repentance and restoration. You are sorry every time you get caught, sorry that your reputation and your life are in ruins, but this is not genuine repentance. The difference between worldly and godly repentance is vital because the two can be easily confused.

Repentance is all about turning towards God. It is possible to be sorry about the consequences of your adultery, while not being truly repentant. A person who is truly repentant turns from his or her sin not with lip service, but with a sincere heart. They then accept responsibility for their actions without conditions. When repentance is genuine it results in forgiveness and reconciliation by the offended party, even if there is pain and an injured heart of your husband or wife. You must take full, not partial, responsibility for your actions. A person who is generally repentant will jump at the opportunity to foster restoration, not expecting anything in return. Your actions reveal the condition of your heart. If you are truly repentant, you'll stop committing adultery because the Bible says, "you shall not commit adultery."

Chapter 3

The Pain of Adultery

In Exodus 20:14 the Bible says: "Thou shalt not commit adultery." If something is commanded not to do anywhere in the bible, it is obvious that it is something God takes very seriously. This does not mean all sins are equal in their severity. Some Christian leaders have proclaimed, "there is no such thing as big sins or little sins, all sins are equal."

This is true in regards to our need for a Savior, Jesus, to pay our sin debt for us. Romans 3:10 says, "For all have sinned and come short of the glory of God."

When presenting the gospel, a good question to ask is, "how many sins does a person have to commit to be a sinner?" Of course, the answer is just one, just like it only takes telling a single lie for you to be a liar. So in that sense, the statement about there being no difference in sin is correct. If a person commits one sin, regardless of what it is, then you will either need to pay the price for that sin, or someone else will have to pay the debt for you. That is the sole reason Jesus, God manifest in the flesh, came to earth to die, be buried and rise again from the dead. He paid a debt he did not owe to purchase us from sin's penalty. Whether we have committed one sin or millions, each have the same sentence, eternal death (Romans 6:23).

That being said, the bible does teach that there are various degrees of severity of sin apart from all warranting the same eternal payment. For example, the bible says in Romans 13, we are to obey all the laws of men, so long as it does not conflict with God's laws and commandments. This means if you are driving 36 MPH in a 35 MPH zone, you have broken the speed limit and sinned by breaking the commandment as found in Romans 13.

However, only a fool would seriously state that this is on an equal with Adolph Hitler killing millions of people. The bible even acknowledges the truth of what I just stated. If you read through the Pentateuch, God lists various penalties for the laws he gives.

"If a man shall steal an ox, or a sheep, and kill it, or sell it; he shall restore five oxen for an ox, and four sheep for a sheep… If the theft be certainly found in his hand alive, whether it be ox, or ass, or sheep; he shall restore double." (Exodus 22:1, 4)

We see here the penalty for the sin of stealing is not prison, but restitution. Now, let's see what the penalty for slavery or human trafficking is.

"And he that stealeth a man, and selleth him, or if he be found in his hand, he shall surely be put to death." (Exodus 21:16)

Notice in this passage, the perpetrator does not kill a person, nor is it even mentioned that he mistreats or assaults a person. If he makes a person a slave, or sells a person as a slave, even if that person is treated decently, the person committing the offense shall be put to death. That is a far cry from what God requires of a thief. This shows that God does not view all sins the same, for if He did they would have the same penalty.

When it comes to the sin of adultery, there are some things worth noting. First, it is the seventh sin in the list of the Ten Commandments.

There were certainly no shortage of sins God could have chosen for the list. In fact, many could argue that slavery is much more deserving on being in the list of ten than something that occurs between "consenting adults."

Secondly, the penalty for adultery in the Old Testament is death. In other words, when it comes to the severity of the consequences, God places adultery in the same list as murder and slavery. This suggests to me that despite the trend in society to view sexual matters as a personal vice rather than a crime, God begs to differ.

Adultery is considered a very serious offense against not just God, but against the wronged spouse. One of the reasons is because Jesus describes the Church, consisting of the body of believers, as his bride that he will one day come to marry. Can you picture the idea of God committing adultery against his bride, like many men do, not just prior to marriage, but in a so-called bachelor party that occurs on the eve of the wedding where all manner of lust, alcohol and women strippers run rampant. How vulgar, disgusting and vile for a person to participate in "one last fling" before marriage. If you participate in such a thing, whether as the groom or a "friend," your morals are that of an alley cat.

Societies views of adultery are the polar opposite of God's views on the matter. Even more importantly, God's feeling on the matter does not change, unlike society which of late treats morals as essentially the equivalent of a fashion trend, changing with the seasons and more a matter of style and taste than absolutes.

Despite people's views of adultery being more accepting towards promiscuity ever since the 1960s in America, ironically, they still cannot get away from the pain adultery brings to a relationship. Even among those who shun Christianity and state they have an "open marriage," they still find themselves feeling hurt and betrayed when their philosophy of free love is put into practice. When the spouse discovers their partner has been "cheating" on them, there will always be some level of betrayal, rejection and humiliation. It brings shame and embarrassment for the faithful spouse.

The word adultery comes from the late Latin word for "to alter, corrupt." Thus, we can see the very foundation of the word has to do with corrupting something that is considered sacred. Later in the book, we will examine other versions of adultery beyond the physical sexual connotations. What is important to note for this section of the book is that when you alter or corrupt something that God intended to be between you and your spouse, you bring pain and anger to them.

Some may try to say adultery is fine because in the bible people like Abraham, David and Solomon had multiple wives and concubines, and since these men are held up as heroes of the faith, why can't we do the same thing?" First, like parents tell their children, "if everyone else jumped off a bridge would you do it?" The idea is the child is supposed to say no, because doing so would kill you. Try using that argument about adultery in a court of law for some other crime and see what happens. "Your honor, you shouldn't throw me in jail for stealing that flat-screen TV because celebrities and politicians steal all the time and never go to jail." You might very well get a snarky answer like, "Yeah, but you aren't them, are you."

The point is, "two wrongs don't make a right." David let the spit run down his beard and clawed at the doors like an animal, pretending to be crazy in 1 Samuel 21, but that doesn't mean we should do the same thing. Nor does God mentioning this account in the bible mean he approved of David's behavior that day. What makes the bible unique is it does not whitewash the sins of its "heroes," unlike worldly books that try to paint a rosy picture of those they worship.

David killed one of his own "mighty men" along with other soldiers to cover up his sin of adultery, and I would challenge anyone to use the same argument justifying their adultery on the basis our leaders in the faith in the bible did it as a justification for committing murder. They would say, "I would never do that." Then why do you do it when it comes to the sexual sin of adultery?

Jesus made it very plain that the patriarchs were not fulfilling God's plans for marriage when they had multiple wives and engaged in polygamy. When the Pharisees asked him about marriage and divorce, this is what he had to say.

"But **from the beginning of the creation** God made them male and female. **For this cause shall a man leave his father and mother, and cleave to his wife**; And they twain shall be one flesh: so then they are no more twain, but one flesh. What therefore God hath joined together, let not man put asunder." (Mark 10:6-9)

In other words, God always intended for marriage to be monogamous. Go back and look at Adam and Eve, you will not find anywhere that Adam had multiple wives. From the Garden of Eden, God decreed that a person's desires should be for your husband or wife. This principle is as inherent in our DNA as a belief in God is (Romans 1:20), and it is for this reason adultery brings pain and betrayal to the offended spouse regardless of their outward professions of spirituality; for deep down, at a level they may not even be aware exists, their DNA tells them something is not right.

It is important to realize that these feelings may express themselves in different ways due to the differences in the way God created men and women. Adam was created to tend the garden and work before the fall or Eve being created. Because of this, when it comes to losing a job, most of the time it is far harder emotionally on men than when a woman gets fired. This is because God created men to work and when they are unemployed, they are not doing the primary thing they were created to do. Of course, I am talking about the physical realm here, for God's greatest desire is for us to walk with Him and serve him, but I am referring to the nuts and bolts of our everyday existence. God made men to work.

Also, God made women different not just in anatomy but in terms of their emotional make-up. Men tend to be more single-minded and focused on the task at hand to where they literally become oblivious to everything going on around them. This is why a man can go hunting and sit in a tree stand for hours at a time with another man, while the temperature is 30 degrees and the two of them never talk the entire time because they are focused on watching for that one deer that may or may not come by. Then at the end of the day, both will say they had a good time. While there may be the rare exception, there is no way a lady could do that and keep quiet and still all that time.

The same is true regarding conversations. Take a group of ladies; they can talk about everything under the sun for an hour with no "dead air" in the conversation. By contrast men can meet someone they haven't seen for a long time and the conversation goes something like this.

"How are you doing"

"Great, how about yourself."

"Oh, not too bad. How's the wife and kids?"

"Doing good. The kids are in high school and my wife just took a new job."

"That's great. Good talking to you."

"Yeah, same to you. I'm glad we got to spend some time together again after all these years."

"Yeah, me too. Good seeing you again."

While this may be a little bit of an exaggeration, let me assure you ladies it is not that far off. Men can talk for just a few minutes and leave thinking they had the best time in the world catching up, compared to women who can talk for hours about every little detail. Please do not misunderstand, this is not meant as any kind of criticism like some do when they joke about "chatty Kathy's" and the like. It is merely an observation. There is a reason people often talk about women gossiping instead of men. This is not to say that men do not and cannot gossip and backbite, trust me, we certainly can. I am merely stating these are general character traits that God used to differentiate the genders. I will be the first to say there are times when a woman's touch is needed to ask for more details about something. This is why God set up the marriage relationship the way he did, for the man and woman to complement each other, not duplicate one another.

Another key difference is women are more emotional, and I don't mean that in a bad sense. By contrast, men tend to just want the problem fixed. By way of example, a man comes home and his wife says, "I had a horrible day today. The sink is clogged up, the computer quit working and the kids are fighting." As men, here is what we think after hearing this. "Ok honey, I'm going to get some liquid plumber and unclog the drain. Then I'll take a look at the computer for you and get it fixed. Afterwards, I'll talk to the kids and tell them to stop fighting."

However, that is not what she is wanting from us. Instead, she wants us to hug her and tell her everything is going to be all right. We look at a situation and think, "how can I fix this," but while she may ultimately want the issue fixed, that is not the primary thing she is desiring at the moment.

The reason I have said all these things is in a marriage relationship it is vital to understand these differences exist and rather than try to change the other spouse, realize this is an innate character trait God created to make men and women different. Once you understand this, you will able to better be able to meet your spouse's needs, for you will understand they are not a clone of you. They respond to the same pressures of life you face in a different way. When it comes to adultery, while feelings of pain and betrayal will affect both parties, they will not necessarily be manifested in the same way.

It is possible for a man to be told his wife has committed adultery and convey very little emotion outwardly, with the exception of anger. He may not cry and fall apart, but rest assured, inwardly, he is hurting just as much as the wife who just found out her husband is cheating on her and is wailing like a banshee.

Because men and women process pain differently, it is vital for the spouse who has done the wrong to give the other spouse time to process what has happened in his or her way. This means exercising extreme patience. Remember, you are the one who committed the misdeed of adultery, so it would be the height of arrogance and presumptuous of you to expect them to react on your terms. Even if you come to them in a spirit of genuine repentance, asking for forgiveness, realize it would be a shock for them to handle it the same way you would. They are not your gender and God made them to be different, so they are going to process what happened differently. This is not to say the concept of forgiveness should not cross gender lines, but it does mean how this forgiveness manifests itself will probably be different than you feel it should be.

Although there is no simple explanation for adultery, one of the biggest comes from neglecting your spiritual life. If you are energized to work but whenever you are home, you are tired and just want to lay down on the couch, you are showing your spouse they are not the most important thing in your life.

Another thing to understand is men and women respond sexually to different stimuli. Men are more attracted to the visual. Women instinctively know this, even if they won't admit it. This is why they will wear a tight-fitting short skirt. It is not to show off the latest fashion to other women, it is to get men to look at them. If a woman has a slit in her dress that reveals her legs as she walks in a kind of "now you see it, now you don't," display, unless a man is walking strongly with the Lord and extremely disciplined, he will find his eyes naturally gravitating towards that direction. This is why David said, "I will put no wicked thing before my eyes." Advertisers know this, for they frequently feature scantily-clad women in ads for products that should have nothing to do with sex. Years ago, Carls Jr., a fast food restaurant featured Paris Hilton in a black wet bikini washing a pickup truck. Please tell me what any of that has to do with buying a hamburger. They know men respond to the visual.

By contrast, women tend to respond more to physical touches than the visual. This is why men will hug a woman at work or put his arm around her. For both men and women, when you realize what stimulates you sexually, you are now armed with the tools to know when you are being manipulated and take steps to avoid it, especially in the workplace.

Men, when you see a pretty woman in the workplace, remember you are always seeing her at her best regarding her appearance. By contrast, your wife cannot possibly look like that all the time, and by the way, that woman you are tempted to have an affair with can't either. I suspect if you saw her with her make-up off you would have a completely different feeling.

Ladies, when you feel a co-worker understands you more than your husband because of a gentle and possibly even an innocuous touch, realize that is just because God made you to be stimulated that way and doesn't need to mean you have to be lulled into an affair.

While the affair is always the fault of the person who made the decision to commit adultery and cheat on their spouse, this does not mean that the other party never bears any of the blame. Again, I am not excusing any immoral behavior, and each person will give an account to God for your own sins, but it is fair to ask the question, did the aggrieved spouse set the other person up to fail, so to speak.

There have been many men who have been married to beautiful women, beauty queens if you will, yet they have affairs with someone who has the face of a horse. On its face this makes no sense, and I am not being unkind to any lady's appearance, all I am saying is to the logical mind it is hard to understand. The reason for the affair has nothing to do with beauty but instead is predicated on the man not getting his romantic needs met at home.

As a result, that tension finds relief in the arms of another woman. I beg of you, please understand I feel that even if this happens at home, the man should have enough character to fight back and not succumb to the temptation. As the leader in the home, men have the responsibility to set the example. I am not justifying the sin of adultery in any way, I am only providing an explanation, not an excuse. I only do this, not to cast blame, but because the sad truth is adultery at its core is a spiritual attack on the institution of marriage, and like in any war, both sides suffer varying degrees of casualties. My burden is to not see either side wounded in this battle, for nobody wins when adultery occurs.

If you are the one committing the adultery, regardless of the reason, understand that while there is pleasure in it for a season, Satan always hides the true cost of sin. Television, advertising and other media portray getting drunk and partying as a fun time, but they never show the hangover with the headache, memory loss as you wonder what you did last night and throwing up. Many an affair began as the result of a drunken party where the inhibitions are lowered. Likewise, Satan and the world emphasizes the physical short-term pleasure that adultery brings, including the thrill of danger, but when the bill comes due, the price is far more expensive than you were told.

Adultery can result in fights that end up in violence, this in turn can lead to having to go to jail or even prison. And of course, I am not even talking about the permanent effects that can come from sexually transmitted diseases. What is tragic is this is not a sin that doesn't hurt anybody. The innocent spouse has the potential to contract a dangerous disease they will bear the rest of their life, despite their not doing anything wrong. During the 1980s, many a wife over in Zambia contracted and died a painful death as a result of their husband's indiscretions. Of course, the same is true in reverse. Even if you repent, you will forever have to live with the reality of what you did to your innocent spouse, who now must bear the scars from your sins for the rest of their life.

That is a painful situation that could cause fights and even jail. Immediately after your husband or wife discovers your adultery but before the healing process can begin, you have to invest your time in your spouse. Turn yourself completely to God. You must deal with the reality of violating the marriage contract. You have to face the consequences of your sins, including the shame, dishonesty and embarrassment that you caused in your marriage. Now you realize that you put your husband or wife in a situation of betrayal, anger and revenge. These will all result in a curse on the marriage relationship.

Let me say, that humanly speaking there is no way to fully restore the damage done to a relationship after these things have been done. The good thing is, God knows that, which is why Jesus says, "without me ye can do nothing" (John 15:5). However, if you have betrayed your spouse, and you turn to God and them in sincere repentance, if you are willing to be humble and patient; understanding that your spouse doesn't owe you anything, through the power of God, the hurt can be healed. It will take time, and you will need to spend lengthy amounts of time in prayer, but God can do all things.

It may take a long time and involve a great deal of spiritual counseling, but it is possible for the marriage to be restored once again. As this begins to occur, I cannot emphasize enough the importance of the one who has committed adultery to do some deep and earnest soul-searching, asking yourself questions in much the same manner a prosecutor would to discover how you arrived at this place in your life. Then you must take an honest assessment to ensure not only that you never do such a betrayal again, but that you do not even come close to giving the appearance of committing adultery.

Remember, regardless of whatever reasons you may feel justified your actions at the time, just like a person who breaks man's law, you must be willing to face the consequences for your actions. When you do that, God will see your humility and honor it.

In 1 Kings 21, Ahab committed the horrible sin of murdering innocent Naboth because he coveted the man's vineyard. Yet, when Elijah confronted Ahab on his sin, Ahab humbled himself and repented of his sin. God was so moved by this act of contrition that he told Elijah to go back and tell Ahab that while he and his family would have to die for his sins, God would do it after Ahab was dead, so he wouldn't have to see his children die. Believe me, that is a big deal, ask any parent who has ever lost a child if you doubt me. The point is, God honors the humble and contrite heart.

You must also be honest enough to understand that while God, being perfect, can completely forgive in an instant, as sinful beings, we do not have that ability. While your spouse may say they forgive you, understand that their statement is most likely just the beginning of the process and it may take months or even years for it to happen completely. This is because the evidence of the trauma is still there, even if the deep hurt is subsiding. Adultery hurts more than you will ever know. Please, stop it before it happens in your marriage. If you are already engaged in adultery, stop it right now.

Chapter 4

How to Repent from Adultery

According the Bible, people who reject Christ and engage in unrepentant adultery will not inherit the kingdom of God. While we are saved by grace through faith (Ephesians 2:8-9), this does not mean works has no part in the life of a Christian. The very next verse states, "For we are his workmanship, created in Christ Jesus unto good works, which God hath before ordained that we should walk in them."

Without going into a deep theological discussion, what is important to understand is that there is a difference between standing and state. When you are born again, you are in God's family and that will not change, no matter what happens. Just like in an earthly family, you are your father's son or daughter no matter what, because that is your state. However, you can do things to harm the relationship between the two of you, and if you sin often enough, your father may even disinherit you, so when he dies all his wealth goes to another. Similarly, Christians have a heavenly inheritance that takes the form of rewards and positions we will have during the millennial reign of Jesus Christ, and afterwards.

"Of the increase of his government and peace there shall be no end, upon the throne of David, and upon his kingdom, to order it, and to establish it with judgment and with justice from henceforth even for ever." (Isaiah 9:6)

When Jesus comes back to earth at the end of the Great Tribulation and sets up his government in Jerusalem, like any government, there are a multitude of positions that will need to be filled. Put simply, what would you rather do in this real physical kingdom, be the mayor of a city or the one in charge of picking up trash? Also, realize that everyone will have an idea of how faithfully you served God in this life by your position. If you are the dog catcher and in charge of cleaning up after their waste, it will be evident you were an unfaithful servant here on earth. I don't know about you, but I don't want to just get into heaven "by the skin of my teeth." Since that is for eternity compared to a miniscule amount of years in this body, I would rather have something worthwhile that I know will last. When it comes to adultery, far too many Christians sell out their inheritance for a mess of pottage like Esau.

Jesus tells us adultery is not the result of outward actions, but always begins in your heart. Matthew 15:19-20a says "For out of the heart proceed evil thoughts, murders, **adulteries, fornications**, thefts, false witness, blasphemies: These are the things which defile a man."

This shows us that in the New Testament, the standard is much higher than in the Old Testament where only the act was prohibited. This does not mean that even then God was not concerned with the heart. David said, "I will set no wicked thing before mine eyes." However, in the Old Testament there was no requirement for a sacrifice for having lustful thoughts. I will also note that there was no sacrifice you could offer for adultery, just like murder it called for capital punishment.

Now, Jesus said even lusting after a woman in your heart is the same as adultery, but of course, we are not calling for the death penalty for that. If we did, the guillotines would be running non-stop. Instead, God calls on us to repent when we have wicked thoughts like adultery.

When we confess it to God, he says he will forgive us of that sin. "If we confess our sins, he is faithful and just to forgive us our sins, and to cleanse us from all unrighteousness" (I John 1:9).

Inherent in the word confess is the idea of repentance. When you confess, you are also admitting what you have done is wrong and a sin against God. Therefore, the most important part of repentance is a change of your heart and your mind. The word repentance means to change your mind. This is also means you have to pray, asking God to change your heart and thoughts. He will give you tools to do so, but it is still your choice whether you listen to the wooing of the Holy Spirit or not when He brings this sin to your attention. Rebuke adulterous thoughts when they enter your mind because the Bible says we are to bring into captivity every thought to the obedience of Christ (2 Corinthians 10:5).

When you change your mind and heart about sin, you will naturally agree with God's will and how he feels about the matter. The Bible says adultery is sin and wickedness, and both believers and nonbelievers should view it as such. By changing your mind and heart you can begin to turn away from the sin of adultery. This will, in turn, enable you to become a faithful wife or husband.

It may seem impossible to overcome adulterous thoughts, but Jesus will give you strength and help you over time. All you have to do is let him lead you to holiness in obedience to God. Once you have repented of adultery, you should immediately act to remove any temptations that would lead you back to this sin.

This does not mean Jesus is calling you to self-mutilate, but the sin of adultery is so serious that you should be willing to take whatever steps are necessary to avoid it and ensure it never happens again. This might mean throwing away your smartphone, computer, and even your television. You may need to stop seeing your old friends or even parents who are loose with their words or dress provocatively to avoid your being tempted with adulterous thoughts.

You would be wise to cut off any and all contact with friends who may entice you to commit adultery. This would include contact via social media, chat rooms and text messaging. If you find yourself attracted to someone, you'd be wise to limit contact with them until you are stronger spiritually. And never allow yourself to be alone with them. I may sound old-fashioned, but I still believe one of the best protections against adultery is to have chaperones. I don't care if you are single and dating someone when you are 50, you should still have another couple or person who takes the responsibility to help the two of you remain pure and chaperone the two of you when you are on a date.

The key is humbling yourself enough to admit you need help, and that includes accountability. A person who thinks they are strong enough never to stumble is setting themselves up for a hard fall. Never flirt with a member of the opposite sex other than your husband or wife. You should take the temptation you have as an opportunity to renew your love for your spouse, placing them above everyone else. Ephesians 5:25 says, "husbands, love your wives, even as Christ also loved the church, and gave himself for it." And in Ephesians 5:22 he said, "Wives, submit yourselves unto your own husbands, as unto the Lord."

If you do engage in adultery, you should immediately come clean with your husband or wife. While this will undoubtedly cause heartache, it is far better they hear it from you than from someone else, or when they begin the experience the symptoms of an STD. Realize that the one cheated will feel hurt and rejected, believing they are unattractive and unloved by their spouse. When they express these emotions to you, it is vital that you do not become defensive, but instead acknowledge you are the one who caused the problem.

But if you are truly repentant, this is the first step to restoring the marriage. Through prayer and biblical counsel, you can survive the sin of adultery and go on to have a happy loving restoration. Healing may take time, but if the adulterer will confess and repent from it, God can and will do wonderful healing.

However, the sad truth is, this will not happen in every case. For many marriages, adultery will end up with a divorce, the parties being unable to reconcile. This is why adultery is such a serious sin. The consequences are so enormous that God's word says divorce is permissible in the case of adultery, even though this is never God's preference in the marriage.

The Bible says any person who divorces and remarries for any reason other than adultery is living in adultery (Matthew 5:32). This verse is more relevant than ever today with the introduction of no-fault divorces in the 1970s. These laws are completely unfair to a spouse who does not desire divorce yet has no legal power to stop it. This poses a problem in light of the above-mentioned verse. As a preacher and teacher, I suggest that since the Bible does not address this issue directly, and you cannot remarry even if there is consent in the marriage, you should honor your current marriage and not seek a divorce.

In fact, many people divorce and remarry sinfully. Jesus said the best way to avoid this dilemma is to forgive the adulterous partner and honor the current remarriage, seeking God's blessing on it. But if divorce occurs under allowable circumstances and neither remarry, reconciliation should be sought if both individuals are willing to do so. If not, and they are Christians, they should remain single for the rest of their lives.

Because of the severity of this scriptural requirement following a divorce, it is absolutely imperative that you realize something about the nature of any sin, especially adultery. The spouse who commits the adultery cannot remarry. This means you will still have those natural sexual desires but will have no outlet to fulfill them. Sin always seems so good on the surface, but the bill is always more than expected, and sin hurts and has killed more people both spiritually and individually than you can imagine. The Bible admits there is pleasure in sin, but warns it is only for a season.

The wisest man who ever lives said, "Stolen waters are sweet, and bread eaten in secret is pleasant" (Proverbs 9:17). When a person begins committing a sin in secret, including adultery, there is a certain rush that comes from it, and you think there is no way you will ever get caught. Not true. Satan wants you to think that, but you should calculate the true cost of sin, which is death.

During a time when David should have been out fighting (2 Samuel 11:1), he saw Bathsheba bathing on her roof and lusted after her. Even though both of them were married, David had her brought to him and slept with her. That was pleasurable for David at the time because he enjoyed himself that evening. After all, the Bible says that in Proverbs 5:3-4, "For the lips of a strange woman drop as an honeycomb, and her mouth is smoother than oil: But her end is bitter as wormwood, sharp as a twoedged sword. Her feet go down to death; her steps take hold on hell."

The pleasure of the sin is for a while and afterwards the hangover comes. When Bathsheba told David she was pregnant, he was eventually forced to have her husband, Uriah, one of David's mighty men, killed, along with several other soldiers to cover up his sin.

There were severe consequences for this sin, even if David was the king. God punished David severely. He vowed that the sword would never depart from David's house and that he would have to repay fourfold. When we look at David's life we see this happened just as God said. First, the baby born from the adulterous relationship died. Next, David's son

Amnon died. The next to die was Absalom and last was David's son Adonijah, who died after David's death at the hand of King Solomon, who was the son of Bathsheba and David. For a parent, there is nothing worse than having to bury one of your children, let alone three of them. Especially when you know it was your sin that killed them.

Not only that, the scripture strongly suggests that David acquired a sexually transmitted disease as a result of his secret sin with Bathsheba.

Psalm 38

A Psalm of David, to bring to remembrance

O LORD, rebuke me not in thy wrath: neither chasten me in thy hot displeasure. For thine arrows stick fast in me, and thy hand presseth me sore. There is no soundness in my flesh because of thine anger; neither is there any rest in my bones because of my sin. For mine iniquities are gone over mine head: as an heavy burden they are too heavy for me. **My wounds stink and are corrupt because of my foolishness.** I am troubled; I am bowed down greatly; I go mourning all the day long. **For my loins are filled with a loathsome disease: and there is no soundness in my flesh.** I am feeble and sore broken: I have roared by reason of the disquietness of my heart. Lord, all my desire is before thee; and my groaning is not hid from thee. My heart panteth, my strength faileth me: as for the light of mine eyes, it also is gone from me. **My lovers and my friends stand aloof from my sore; and my kinsmen stand afar off.** They also that seek after my life lay snares for me: and they that seek my hurt speak mischievous things, and imagine deceits all the day long. But I, as a deaf man, heard not; and I was as a dumb man that openeth not his mouth.

(Psalm 38:1-13)

There is no record in scripture that David was ever healed of this disease, meaning he had to bear the consequences of his sin, including the horrible smell associated with it, for the rest of his life. Whenever he conducted a meeting with anyone, including his trusted aides, the smell filled the room, reminding all of those present what David had done.

While this may seem sad and depressing, there is also a wonderful picture of God's grace in this. In the Old Testament there were two sins that were punishable by death and no sacrifice could be offered to obtain forgiveness; these sins were murder and adultery. When David was presented with his sin by Nathan the prophet, he immediately went to God in sincere repentance just before God was about to kill him. As a result of his genuine penitence, God spared David's life.

God said David was "a man after mine own heart" (Acts 13:22). This doesn't seem to make sense in view of the sins David committed. However, it is worth noting that while David messed up many times in his life, whenever he was confronted with it, he never hesitated to quickly bring it to God in a spirit of sincere repentance. In other words, he kept short accounts with God. I believe what God is saying is that literally, David was a man who sought after God's own heart by always wanting to ensure the bond of fellowship was never broken for very long.

If you are stuck with the sin of adultery, I want you to repent of your sins and turn to Jesus. Because Jesus died for your sins, he is able to cleanse you with his blood, forgive you and lead you to the power of the Holy Spirit. Adultery goes against God's plan for the family, God's plan for the marriage is to be holy in unity and love. Adultery is a wicked sin of your heart and brings serious consequences. You may seem to think that an innocent flirtation or an explicit text message will be fine, and you will get away with it, but this is not true.

"Behold, ye have sinned against the LORD: **and be sure your sin will find you out."** (Numbers 32:23)

Chapter 5

Adultery Costs More Than You Think

Adultery is a very serious sin against God and your spouse. Outside of death, it is the worst nightmare a faithful husband or wife can experience. The primary reason is, beyond the sinful aspect of the behavior, adultery is a betrayal of the trust both parties entered into when they left their families to enter into the bond of marriage and become one flesh. It is not uncommon for adultery to end up in a divorce. In America today, the laws regarding the terms of a divorce such as child custody arrangements, alimony, child support, and the splitting up of assets strongly favors the woman, regardless of which one is the guilty party. The court is supposed to take into consideration which party is responsible for the divorce and determine the amount of alimony and child support to the faithful spouse in a fair manner, but judgments are almost always in favor of the wife. When arriving at its ruling, the court can consider extenuating factors such as adultery or marital misconduct.

Adultery occurs when a married man or woman has sexual relations with someone other than their spouse. Jesus' words on this subject leaves us no doubt how harmful adultery can. However, praise God, even in the midst of this dark news, Jesus does not leave us hopeless; he also talks of grace and mercy from a loving God. Often adulterers wonder about forgiveness, divorce, and its consequences. While you can obtain forgiveness if you are sincere in your repentance, there are some things that can never be undone.

A story was told many years ago of a boy who did bad things growing up. They were not evil, but more mischievous than anything else, but they still hurt people. To help him understand the consequences of his sin, the boy's father made him pound a nail halfway into a fence anytime he did something wrong. After several weeks, the boy lamented that there was no more room for nails. The father then told him, "for every good thing you do, you can remove a nail." The boy was excited and went around helping people and doing good. Soon, he was able to remove the last nail from the fence.

"Dad, look. I've removed the last nail. I'm so excited."

"Good job, son," the father said.

"But dad, the fence has all these holes in it from where the nails used to be."

"That's right son. That is what sin does to a person. You can get forgiveness from God and remove the nail of that particular sin, but it always leaves a mark."

The bible not only commands us not to commit adultery, it contains many warnings regarding the cause of adultery and gives us ways to avoid it.

"Flee also youthful lusts…" (2 Timothy 2:22)

"But whoso committeth adultery with a woman lacketh understanding: he that doeth it destroyeth his own soul." (Proverbs 6:32)

"Marriage is honourable in all, and the bed undefiled: but whoremongers and adulterers God will judge." (Hebrews 13:4)

"And Jesus said, Are ye also yet without understanding? Do not ye yet understand, that whatsoever entereth in at the mouth goeth into the belly, and is cast out into the draught? But those things which proceed out of the mouth come forth from the heart; and they defile the man. **For out of the heart proceed** evil thoughts, murders, adulteries, **fornications**, thefts, false witness, blasphemies: **These are the things which defile a man**: but to eat with unwashen hands defileth not a man." (Matthew 15:16-20)

"I have seen thine adulteries, and thy neighings, the lewdness of thy whoredom, and thine abominations on the hills in the fields. Woe unto thee, O Jerusalem! wilt thou not be made clean? when shall it once be?" (Jeremiah 13:27)

Repent of your sin and you will live. In 1 John 1:9 it says, "If we confess our sins, he is faithful and just to forgive us our sins, and to cleanse us from all unrighteousness."

"Whosoever putteth away his wife, and marrieth another, committeth adultery: and whosoever marrieth her that is put away from her husband committeth adultery." (Luke 16:18)

The bible position on when divorce is or is not permitted is quite clear in this area and there is no ambiguity. In the old Testament men were known to divorce a wife at "the drop of a hat," or for any reason at all. However, Jesus tells us under the new covenant following Calvary, you cannot divorce your wife just because she disrespects you or she cannot cook and clean, or any of the other frivolous reasons we see today. In Matthew 19:9 Jesus said, "And I say unto you, Whosoever shall put away his wife, except it be for fornication, and shall marry another, committeth adultery: and whoso marrieth her which is put away doth commit adultery."

By God's law a married woman is bound to her husband so long as he is alive, but if her husband dies, she is free from the law that binds her to him and is able to remarry. If she has sexual relations with another man while her husband is still alive, she is an adulteress. But if her husband commits adultery she is free to marry another man.

Adultery is a very serious sin before God's eyes. By committing it, you are saying you are more concerned about the affairs of this world rather than the sacred vows you took. For the married woman, your desire should be to please your husband only, not another man. I am saying this for your own good, so you may live in a right way with an undivided devotion to the Lord. If you're worried that you might not be acting honorably toward your marriage and your passions for your husband are not what they should be, you need to pray for God to give you a strong desire and passion for your husband. If you are not a believer and are willing to live with your husband, you should not commit adultery. Otherwise the consequences will be severe.

Whether you are a believer or unbeliever, you should trust the Lord in whatever situation the Lord has placed you in. When God called you, you become a slave because you "are bought with a price" (1 Corinthians 7:23). God is your master, do not become the slave of sin. The devil and the deeds of the wicked ensnare you, the courts of your sin hold you fast. The only one God permits a person to have any type of sexual relations with is your spouse.

Adultery will cost you far more than you ever imagined. It could cost you your reputation, your job, your marriage, your kids, your health, your finances, and bring about divorce, lawsuits, alimony payments and child support. Not to mention the cost on your spiritual life, and so much more. You do not have any authority over your own body but are instead to yield it to your spouse, not any other person. In the same way, your husband does not have authority over his own body but is commanded to yield it to you, not someone else. Now, you are to come together again so Satan will not tempt you because of your lack of self-control.

The Apostle Paul had a great deal of wisdom to offer regarding how to avoid falling into fornication and adultery.

1 Corinthians 7:1-39

(1) Now concerning the things whereof ye wrote unto me: It is good for a man not to touch a woman.

(2) Nevertheless, to avoid fornication, let every man have his own wife, and let every woman have her own husband.

(3) Let the husband render unto the wife due benevolence: and likewise also the wife unto the husband.

(4) The wife hath not power of her own body, but the husband: and likewise also the husband hath not power of his own body, but the wife.

(5) Defraud ye not one the other, except it be with consent for a time, that ye may give yourselves to fasting and prayer; and come together again, that Satan tempt you not for your incontinency.

(6) But I speak this by permission, and not of commandment.

(7) For I would that all men were even as I myself. But every man hath his proper gift of God, one after this manner, and another after that.

(8) I say therefore to the unmarried and widows, It is good for them if they abide even as I.

(9) But if they cannot contain, let them marry: for it is better to marry than to burn.

(10) And unto the married I command, yet not I, but the Lord, Let not the wife depart from her husband:

(11) But and if she depart, let her remain unmarried, or be reconciled to her husband: and let not the husband put away his wife.

(12) But to the rest speak I, not the Lord: If any brother hath a wife that believeth not, and she be pleased to dwell with him, let him not put her away.

(13) And the woman which hath an husband that believeth not, and if he be pleased to dwell with her, let her not leave him.

(14) For the unbelieving husband is sanctified by the wife, and the unbelieving wife is sanctified by the husband: else were your children unclean; but now are they holy.

(15) But if the unbelieving depart, let him depart. A brother or a sister is not under bondage in such cases: but God hath called us to peace.

(16) For what knowest thou, O wife, whether thou shalt save thy husband? or how knowest thou, O man, whether thou shalt save thy wife?

(17) But as God hath distributed to every man, as the Lord hath called every one, so let him walk. And so ordain I in all churches.

(18) Is any man called being circumcised? let him not become uncircumcised. Is any called in uncircumcision? let him not be circumcised.

(19) Circumcision is nothing, and uncircumcision is nothing, but the keeping of the commandments of God.

(20) Let every man abide in the same calling wherein he was called.

(21) Art thou called being a servant? care not for it: but if thou mayest be made free, use it rather.

(22) For he that is called in the Lord, being a servant, is the Lord's freeman: likewise also he that is called, being free, is Christ's servant.

(23) Ye are bought with a price; be not ye the servants of men.

(24) Brethren, let every man, wherein he is called, therein abide with God.

(25) Now concerning virgins I have no commandment of the Lord: yet I give my judgment, as one that hath obtained mercy of the Lord to be faithful.

(26) I suppose therefore that this is good for the present distress, I say, that it is good for a man so to be.

(27) Art thou bound unto a wife? seek not to be loosed. Art thou loosed from a wife? seek not a wife.

(28) But and if thou marry, thou hast not sinned; and if a virgin marry, she hath not sinned. Nevertheless such shall have trouble in the flesh: but I spare you.

(29) But this I say, brethren, the time is short: it remaineth, that both they that have wives be as though they had none;

(30) And they that weep, as though they wept not; and they that rejoice, as though they rejoiced not; and they that buy, as though they possessed not;

(31) And they that use this world, as not abusing it: for the fashion of this world passeth away.

(32) But I would have you without carefulness. He that is unmarried careth for the things that belong to the Lord, how he may please the Lord:

(33) But he that is married careth for the things that are of the world, how he may please his wife.

(34) There is difference also between a wife and a virgin. The unmarried woman careth for the things of the Lord, that she may be holy both in body and in spirit: but she that is married careth for the things of the world, how she may please her husband.

(35) And this I speak for your own profit; not that I may cast a snare upon you, but for that which is comely, and that ye may attend upon the Lord without distraction.

(36) But if any man think that he behaveth himself uncomely toward his virgin, if she pass the flower of her age, and need so require, let him do what he will, he sinneth not: let them marry.

(37) Nevertheless he that standeth stedfast in his heart, having no necessity, but hath power over his own will, and hath so decreed in his heart that he will keep his virgin, doeth well.

(38) So then he that giveth her in marriage doeth well; but he that giveth her not in marriage doeth better.

(39) The wife is bound by the law as long as her husband liveth; but if her husband be dead, she is at liberty to be married to whom she will; only in the Lord.

King Solomon, who was the wisest man who ever lived, and is also known as "the preacher," had some excellent advice as well.

Proverbs 5:1-23

(1) My son, attend unto my wisdom, and bow thine ear to my understanding:

(2) That thou mayest regard discretion, and that thy lips may keep knowledge.

(3) For the lips of a strange woman drop as an honeycomb, and her mouth is smoother than oil:

(4) But her end is bitter as wormwood, sharp as a twoedged sword.

(5) Her feet go down to death; her steps take hold on hell.

(6) Lest thou shouldest ponder the path of life, her ways are moveable, that thou canst not know them.

(7) Hear me now therefore, O ye children, and depart not from the words of my mouth.

(8) Remove thy way far from her, and come not nigh the door of her house:

(9) Lest thou give thine honour unto others, and thy years unto the cruel:

(10) Lest strangers be filled with thy wealth; and thy labours be in the house of a stranger;

(11) And thou mourn at the last, when thy flesh and thy body are consumed,

(12) And say, How have I hated instruction, and my heart despised reproof;

(13) And have not obeyed the voice of my teachers, nor inclined mine ear to them that instructed me!

(14) I was almost in all evil in the midst of the congregation and assembly.

(15) Drink waters out of thine own cistern, and running waters out of thine own well.

(16) Let thy fountains be dispersed abroad, and rivers of waters in the streets.

(17) Let them be only thine own, and not strangers' with thee.

(18) Let thy fountain be blessed: and rejoice with the wife of thy youth.

(19) Let her be as the loving hind and pleasant roe; let her breasts satisfy thee at all times; and be thou ravished always with her love.

(20) And why wilt thou, my son, be ravished with a strange woman, and embrace the bosom of a stranger?

(21) For the ways of man are before the eyes of the LORD, and he pondereth all his goings.

(22) His own iniquities shall take the wicked himself, and he shall be holden with the cords of his sins.

(23) He shall die without instruction; and in the greatness of his folly he shall go astray.

Proverbs 6:20-35

(20) My son, keep thy father's commandment, and forsake not the law of thy mother:

(21) Bind them continually upon thine heart, and tie them about thy neck.

(22) When thou goest, it shall lead thee; when thou sleepest, it shall keep thee; and when thou awakest, it shall talk with thee.

(23) For the commandment is a lamp; and the law is light; and reproofs of instruction are the way of life:

(24) To keep thee from the evil woman, from the flattery of the tongue of a strange woman.

(25) Lust not after her beauty in thine heart; neither let her take thee with her eyelids.

(26) For by means of a whorish woman a man is brought to a piece of bread: and the adulteress will hunt for the precious life.

(27) Can a man take fire in his bosom, and his clothes not be burned?

(28) Can one go upon hot coals, and his feet not be burned?

(29) So he that goeth in to his neighbour's wife; whosoever toucheth her shall not be innocent.

(30) Men do not despise a thief, if he steal to satisfy his soul when he is hungry;

(31) But if he be found, he shall restore sevenfold; he shall give all the substance of his house.

(32) But whoso committeth adultery with a woman lacketh understanding: he that doeth it destroyeth his own soul.

(33) A wound and dishonour shall he get; and his reproach shall not be wiped away.

(34) For jealousy is the rage of a man: therefore he will not spare in the day of vengeance.

(35) He will not regard any ransom; neither will he rest content, though thou givest many gifts.

Because God hates adultery Paul warned us about its dangers.

1 Corinthians 6:9-20

(9) Know ye not that the unrighteous shall not inherit the kingdom of God? Be not deceived: neither fornicators, nor idolaters, nor adulterers, nor effeminate, nor abusers of themselves with mankind,

(10) Nor thieves, nor covetous, nor drunkards, nor revilers, nor extortioners, shall inherit the kingdom of God.

(11) And such were some of you: but ye are washed, but ye are sanctified, but ye are justified in the name of the Lord Jesus, and by the Spirit of our God.

(12) All things are lawful unto me, but all things are not expedient: all things are lawful for me, but I will not be brought under the power of any.

(13) Meats for the belly, and the belly for meats: but God shall destroy both it and them. Now the body is not for fornication, but for the Lord; and the Lord for the body.

(14) And God hath both raised up the Lord, and will also raise up us by his own power.

(15) Know ye not that your bodies are the members of Christ? shall I then take the members of Christ, and make them the members of an harlot? God forbid.

(16) What? know ye not that he which is joined to an harlot is one body? for two, saith he, shall be one flesh.

(17) But he that is joined unto the Lord is one spirit.

(18) Flee fornication. Every sin that a man doeth is without the body; but he that committeth fornication sinneth against his own body.

(19) What? know ye not that your body is the temple of the Holy Ghost which is in you, which ye have of God, and ye are not your own?

(20) For ye are bought with a price: therefore glorify God in your body, and in your spirit, which are God's.

Most people understand that adultery is sin. Even those who want nothing to do with God instinctively know there is something wrong with it, and even today it carries a certain stigma among society at large. We see this in the news cycle with all the stories on President Donald Trump and his one-time act of adultery with "Stormy Daniels" over twelve years ago. Even politicians and reporters who eschew biblical morality have criticized this affair. Their statements validate that we are created with a natural instinct to know adultery is wrong, even though some try to suppress these feelings. We all understand how marriages have been destroyed by the sin of adultery. Sin has never been tolerated by God, neither should not it be tolerated by the church.

The wronged party goes through a plethora of emotions upon discovering they have been betrayed. It is one thing to be betrayed by co-workers or even friends, but when the betrayal comes from your spouse, who should be your closest confidant, it creates a wound that has the potential to be mortal. The two of you made vows so sacred, God intended for them to be only said between a couple for life. These vows are publicly proclaimed before a pastor and those attending your wedding who witness the proclaiming of your vows.

These vows are even more serious than the oath one takes in a courtroom to tell the truth. Now, one of the members has perjured themselves before God, and the spouse learns the horrible news. The aggrieved party has been betrayed by the one they vowed to love and cherish, in sickness and in health, in poverty as in wealth, and forsaking all others, keeping themselves only onto the other spouse, so long as both of you shall live, till death do you part. Upon hearing these vows are now meaningless by the other spouse, the wronged party will feel shocked, angry, filled with doubt, depressed and worst of all, living a life in deep pain.

For the one committing the adultery, knowing your sin has been found out will hopefully cause you to ask a multitude of questions. Among these are, "how can I claim to love my spouse and then do something like this? Were they not good enough for me, despite my claims to the contrary on our wedding day?" Having these invasive, repetitive thoughts about what went on during the time of your adulterous affair can be used for great good if you will deal with it in an honest and forthright manner.

By doing an honest circumspection between you and God, while there will still be consequences, it can provide you with a way to try and take control of your life that is clearly broken and in chaos. The gospel of Jesus Christ is the hope of you in every way of your life. Without this wonderful gift of Jesus Christ, you will never be a person of value. The issue of adultery will leave you with absolutely no hope at all. The sin of adultery is never to be taken lightly. All your sins condemn you before the holy God, but remember that Jesus Christ is your hope. He came to this world to save sinners like you and me. When Jesus died on the cross, he took on himself the sins of all who would repent. So confess your sins to Jesus and take him as your Lord by faith. When you do, you will be free from the bondage of adultery because the Bible tells all sinners like you and me to "repent," or turn to God. Confessing your sins to the Lord is necessary for your salvation, even the sin of adultery can be forgiven.

The apostle Paul spoke of the forgiveness of "all sin." He quoted David who wrote in the Psalms, "Blessed are they whose iniquities are forgiven, and whose sins are covered."

"If we confess our sins, he is faithful and just to forgive us our sins, and to cleanse us from all unrighteousness." (1 John 1:9)

A believer must confess the sin of adultery to the Lord, repent of that sin then "go and sin no more."

Jesus said that to the woman who was caught in the very act of adultery. All sin is counted as unrighteousness before God. He is holy and pure, and he cannot tolerate sin or excuse any sin without executing punishment. Keep in mind despite being forgiven, she remained an adulterer for the rest of her life, the difference was she was forgiven and no longer committed this sin. In John 8:11, Jesus said to the woman "go, and sin no more."

Even if Jesus did not condemn her, he can't excuse or tolerate her sin of adultery. Adultery is always a sin of passion and this is true for Christians and non-Christians. Anyone in life can fall into that kind of sin, from members of the church, politicians, kings, generals, movie stars, the rich and the pauper.

Sadly, this sin frequently shatters the lives of the children who find themselves broken and battered by the storm of adultery. There is nothing good about adultery, and God does not offer you even the slightest excuse to ever commit this deadly sin against God and your spouse.

When God spoke the words, "you shall not commit adultery," he was establishing that any sexual activity between a man and woman outside of the marriage covenant is adultery. In so doing, God affirmed that the marriage relationship was to remain sacred, and the marriage covenant between a man and a woman should reflect that faithfulness. God wants you to remain faithful to the marriage just as he remains faithful to you. In the evil world that you live in, God is honest and just.

The Greek words for commit and commits come from the root words Δεσμευτούν and Δεσμεύει. In John 8, the first word is in the aorist passive tense, meaning that the act of committing adultery is completed and done against the woman. This would suggest that you commit adultery when you have sexual relations with someone other than your husband or your wife (Matthew 19:9; Mark 10:10-11:12; Luke 16:18).

The second word Δεσμεύει is in the present tense, meaning that the woman in the relationship also commits adultery and by flesh joining flesh, she has in effect married the one she committed adultery with. For the innocent spouse, the bible reveals that the woman can live in a state of non-adultery so long as she does not marry again. Even if her husband marries someone else, she or he remains an adulterer according to Romans 7:3.

"So then if, while her husband liveth, she be married to another man, she shall be called an adulteress: but if her husband be dead, she is free from that law; so that she is no adulteress, though she be married to another man." (Romans 7:3)

Why are you still adulterers? Because God says you should not have been married in the first place. Even though you are forgiven of your sins, you are still an adulterer. Yes, adultery is forgiven, but that does not change what has occurred. A person who tells a single lie is forever a liar, and similarly the words adultery, adulterer and adulterous describes the type of sin just as liar describes false statements. You must never forget that God hates both adultery (Malachi 2:14) and lying (Proverbs 6:16-19).

So the effect of this sin is just like any other sin; there are always unavoidable consequences. But don't forget that God forgives the sin of adultery. He forgave David who committed adultery. Infidelity creates a very different difficult and painful situation. Go to the Lord for comfort. He can equip you through the deepest of trials. Adultery is always wrong. Adultery will judge the adulterer and all those who commit sexual immorality.

Seek the Lord to help you in prayer for guidance. Pray for the offender, pray for yourself, and the Lord will direct your thoughts. The betrayer is going to suffer the effects of deep hurt. It is normal to feel anger and hurt caused by adultery. Bringing these emotions to God is the first step towards healing. Giving your emotions and needs to God allows him to minister to your heart so you can begin to let go of the offense and seek a Christian counselor. You should be willing to extend forgiveness to the adulterer. This forgiveness may not be accomplished for some time, but the willingness should always be present. You must consider the possibility that the unfaithful wife or husband will not repent of her or his sin. Understand, forgiveness is not forgetting. You are not asked to forget the experience but to deal with it and move on with your life. Sin has natural consequences, and even those who are forgiven may continue to suffer. Forgiveness is not the elimination of consequences, forgiveness is not a feeling, it is a commitment to pardon the adulterer. Forgiveness is not a private matter or secret act within one individual. This is why confession and repentance need to occur. Forgiveness is not the immediate restoration of trust. Don't think when you've forgiven an unfaithful wife or husband it means everything is back to normal the next day. Rebuilding trust and only begins after a process of reconciliation involving true repentance and a time of proving yourself.

Forgiveness may be offered by the adulterer, but to be complete it requires that the adulterer acknowledge their need for forgiveness, and following repentance, starts over in the relationship. When a marriage is in a state of crisis you should ask God to help you see how to manage the anger and feelings. The Holy Spirit will enable you to do it you could not do on your own. You can do all things through God who gives you strength. True forgiveness and reconciliation are possible. No matter how long it takes, ask God to lead you. Every effort must be made to forgive and reconcile. As to whether to stay in the marriage or not, even if you have biblical grounds for divorce, remember God's preferences are forgiveness and reconciliation.

In John 8:1-11, a woman caught in adultery was brought to Jesus. The religious leaders of the day wanted him to uphold their law that called for capital punishment by stoning her. It was noted that she was caught "in the very act."

Jesus did not speak a single word to them, but just started writing on the ground. Being the incarnate Word, he knew exactly what the scripture said on this matter. I suspect Jesus was writing Deuteronomy 22:22. "If a man be found lying with a woman married to an husband, **then they shall both of them die,** both the man that lay with the woman, and the woman: so shalt thou put away evil from Israel."

Jesus knew exactly what they were trying to do, so with the words of Deuteronomy 22:22 on the ground, Jesus embarrassed them by saying "whosoever had no sin, let him cast the first stone."

This was very significant because the Old Testament law they were citing as the basis for stoning this woman called for both the man and the woman to be put to death. Since she was caught in the very act of adultery, this begs the question, where was the man? This seems to imply that even though the woman was a known adulterous, she was set up by the Pharisees to trick Jesus and see what he would do. However, knowing their hearts he knew there was no one innocent in this crowd, hence his statement.

The reason no one picked up a stone and all left was because they clearly understood they were all sinners and Jesus had their number. The law called for the death penalty for both the woman and the man convicted of adultery and the law was established by God.

This begs the question; can you commit adultery and remain unpunished. In the Old Testament adultery was punishable by death.

That punishment does not apply today, but adultery still carries a stigma and has significant consequences. Full grace can be found in Jesus by repenting. Jesus said, "For God sent not his Son into the world to condemn the world; but that the world through him might be saved."

The consequence of adultery will remain, but the punishment is taken away by the death of Jesus Christ on the cross.

Chapter 6

Adultery Destroys Marriages

You admit to committing adultery in your marriage and know that you would never be caught. Adultery is only a sin against your husband or wife, you reason to yourself, but the act is an attack on the very institution of marriage, which God established as a sacred covenant. Because of this, adultery can cause grave consequences, for is not just a sin against the individual but against God. It is the most destructive conduct in a relationship. It exists because humans have decided that their way is better than God's way. They decided to commit adultery to fulfill their own desires rather than obeying and glorifying their God.

You must hear what the Bible says about adultery order to see it the way God sees it. The Bible says, "you shall not commit adultery." God gave us these laws to make us holy. If you ever think that God takes this or any other sin lightly, you should remember the penalties and punishment he assigned to them to get an idea of how God feels about the severity of them.

Despite what our society would tell us today, adultery is not a simple action between two consenting adults that harms no one. God warns against adultery over and over because he knows the devastating effects adultery has on a marriage and families. He is not a mean God that doesn't want us to have any fun, instead he wants to protect us from the heartbreak that he knows will result as a natural consequence of this sin.

Adultery will keep you away from the kingdom of God and prevent you from having the type of fellowship he intended for you to enjoy with him. The apostle Paul says in first Corinthians 6:9-10, "Know ye not that the unrighteous shall not inherit the kingdom of God? Be not deceived: neither fornicators, nor idolaters, nor adulterers, nor effeminate, nor abusers of themselves with mankind, nor thieves, nor covetous, nor drunkards, nor revilers, nor extortioners, shall inherit the kingdom of God."

This passage further emphasizes how serious God views the sin of adultery. You should never let sin dwell in your mind. Instead you should always stay in God's will. You should not try to cover up your sin; you should repent and seek God's forgiveness when you stumble and fall. God even forgives the sin of adultery. He offers forgiveness when you come to faith in Jesus Christ by confessing and repenting of your sin. God is a faithful God. He will forgive all your sins. All you have to do to become a new creation is no longer desire to be helpless to resist temptation, but yearn to be empowered by the Holy Spirit. Whether the sin is adultery or something else, Jesus Christ has paid the price for you to be forgiven by his death on the cross. There is no such thing as a person who has committed too much sin for God to forgive, but you must be willing to repent and turn to God to receive this free offer of forgiveness that he makes available to everybody who is willing to confess and repent of their sins.

The Bible contains the truth that God wants you to base your spiritual life on. But only when you yield your life to the words of God can you do this. Adultery is a lack of concern for your duty as a wife or husband.

Previously, you may have witnessed to many people, testifying about Jesus Christ and explaining how he saved you, while going over the plan of salvation and stressing the urgency of their making a decision on the issue. But now, you have come to learn that one of those you witnessed to learned of your adultery and did not feel he needed to be saved because at least he has been faithful to his wife, so how could God possibly send him to hell while allowing you into heaven. So you cannot help but wonder how many others have also turned from the offer to seek the truth of the Word of God you shared with them, disregarding what you shared because of your adultery and hypocritical lifestyle.

So what is it you want to please yourself and others with rather than God in your marriage commitment, rather than considering the way to deal with your adultery. You cannot just agree to the biblical remedy, which is the death penalty. Take a moment and think about the feelings of the aggrieved party.

They probably are confused, wondering why you would do such a thing. "I love you. I invested in you by attempting to follow the word of God to the best of my ability to be the spouse God instructs me to be."

Faced with all this, you are certainly unclear as to why you stepped out and committed adultery, especially when you remind yourself of all the times the Lord warned you about this sin through his instructions in the Bible. He especially showed you that as a believer you are held to a higher standard than someone who does not know the Lord because, as it is written, "to whom much is given, much is required." God brings to your remembrance that while people have always engaged in adultery, including God's people, it will more prevalent by everyone at the end of this age.

This know also, that in the last days perilous times shall come. For men shall be lovers of their own selves, covetous, boasters, proud, blasphemers, disobedient to parents, unthankful, unholy, Without natural affection, trucebreakers, false accusers, incontinent, fierce, despisers of those that are good, Traitors, heady, highminded, lovers of pleasures more than lovers of God; Having a form of godliness, but denying the power thereof: from such turn away. (2 Timothy 3:1-5)

Sometimes ask yourself if the excuses the world offers to not just justify, but seem to require a person to be promiscuous, will be beneficial to your marriage. Instead, when you commit adultery, you are acting in ways that actually remove the protective covering from sexual sin God has provided through the relation a wife and husband share with each other.

Rather than keep sex within the bounds of marriage, you chose to disregard the way God established intimacy to be between a couple. Rather than follow the example of Jesus, when he was tempted in the wilderness and the devil chided him to prove that he was the son of God by acting outside the provision of the will of his Father, responded "man shall not live by bread alone, but by every word that proceedeth out of the mouth of God," you decided to give in to your fleshly desires. You cannot claim that God does not know what it is like to be tempted with the desires of the flesh, for the bible says Jesus was "tempted like as we are."

Rather than yield to the temptation to commit adultery, what if, by staying true to your vows, even in this situation, you were to realize that by resisting, it allows you to show your husband that you still regard him as your covenant spouse, and you are determined to honor your vows that were made, not just to your husband or wife on your wedding day, but to God.

It seems to be the wisest thing for you to do at present would be to stop committing adultery. It will hurt your spouse and your children. When you took these vows, you made them for life. "In sickness as in health; in poverty as in wealth, and forsaking all others, so long as you both shall live, till death do you part."

Unlike earthy contracts that are allowed to be changed, or that one party choses to disregard on a whim, those vows are still in effect. Saying what you mean and meaning what you say has power. Even God takes note of the power contained in the words of the wedding vows, and he honors and blesses the person who keeps their own words. It used to be a great value to be known as a wife of your word like the woman of Proverbs 31.

Following the recitation of your marriage vows, and with the conclusion of the marriage ceremony, there is a certain expectation that you are to be trusted and you have been entrusted with great value and character. Yet this place and position of great honor can be torn down and reduced to bubble in an instant. These are two of the consequences of your adultery. As the Bible says, at the end of this age there will be an increase of knowledge and people will run to and fro (Daniel 12:4). The problem is, while mankind has access to more knowledge than at any time in our history, we do very little with it. Instead, we are ever learning and never able to come to the knowledge of the truth (2 Timothy 3:7). This is true in the area of adultery as well. Nearly everyone knows that adultery is wrong, even those who are lost. Yet, they disregard this knowledge and willingly commit this sin anyway because society and the media has worked overtime to remove the stigma attached to it.

In the 1950s, on the television show, *I Love Lucy*, the couple were shown having separate beds because in real life they were not married at the time. My, how things have changed. If you have committed adultery, you have broken the vow you made and perjured yourself before heaven. This makes you a liar and a betrayer. The question now is, what are you going to do about it? Are you going to choose to do the will of your God which is in heaven, or will you continue to do the will of Satan who tells you that adultery is okay?

The bible says you shall not commit adultery. When it occurs you feel stripped, all by yourself and your will is broken. If it was a one-time thing, you must stop it immediately by confessing that this was not ongoing adultery, but it is still sin. You know the scripture, the warnings against uniting your flesh with a married man or woman are found throughout the book of Proverbs, yet while in that phase of sexual immorality, you went ahead and did the act. Now, you realize your stupid foolish selfish act, which you cannot take back. You wept and wept in the conviction of the Holy Spirit and still feel sorrow. The only way to survive these thoughts is to use the power of God like a wave, where it crashes one upon another. This is like your faith.

Sometimes, the only place for you to regain your position to where you can be useful again following loss or challenges is to consistently rest in Jesus Christ. You have many blessings in your marriage, your husband, your nice house, car, security, and you are working. You don't pay any bills, but despite having all these things, you are not happy because you are not sure what contentment and happiness really are. You know the scripture which says, happy is the wife whose God is the Lord. You have all of what life says is important regarding your marital needs and more, but you are still not happy. You crave your husband's time and attention, but seek after contentment from other things, not letting him know about your discontentment. You offer encouraging words to your husband while sustaining your lack of being a good wife by way of practicing thankfulness and considering that he might be overworked and tired.

Instead, you became a flirty woman, texting other men in their houses while they sleeps alone in the other room. He cannot stand to go through the pain and suffering you have caused. The ongoing rejection of his obedient absence comes up from time to time throughout the day and very much before bedtime. Contentment is just not the same thing as happiness.

You are sad, but the experiences are a measure of being in the love and care of another man who is a married man. The life you are fighting to live within is further challenged by the ongoing daily reality of adultery which will destroy your life and soul.

You need to renew your mind in order to submit your husband and then come by way of growing in the knowledge of all that God has addressed to everyone, and especially to you so that you do not harm your life, family and others. Everything God commands is not only good for you to think about, it is vital if you are to learn and grow in your ability to perform the deep spiritual knowledge that comes from walking in all that those who have his wisdom can do.

For those who come to Christ, there is no longer any excuse to live falsely. One of the biggest damages adultery of this magnitude does is to cause you to realize that your whole life with the relationship of someone else's husband or wife is a false one. You know that the things you have lived through make up the life that you have experienced, but you also know that your husband is the man that God will reveal in your life, but you did not care. Instead, you ignored the person God created just for you and rather than grow in knowledge of him, you decided to connect with a man who has children of his own that you met on the job. You only see him at his best, regarding his appearance and how he carries himself in public, never seeing all the "warts" he has underneath it all, like you do with your husband.

Only seeing the part of him that he wants to reveal to you, you approached him and made the decision to begin that illicit relationship. Even if you are married, from the first time the two of you meet for your first date, you began plotting how to sneak around and have this secret relationship for the long haul. You know it is wrong, but you are unsure what to do, feeling the situation is so difficult it is hard to get your head around. This confusion prevents you from coming to your senses and deciding to take control of your life.

While you may achieve some temporary fleshly pleasure, it will soon disappear when the moment passes, and you come back to your normal life. You may gain short-term satisfaction, but the loss of all the good things God has provided you for your marriage and your family attempts to drive you to become repentant and embrace the truth. When this happens, it is vital that you heed the wooing of the Holy Spirit. Your soul is on the line. You have heard enough truth to believe, but you have chosen not to seek the truth. You heard the word of God for many years, but rather than submit and obey, you are deceived by your own lusts, which causes you to feed the flesh rather than obtain nourishment from the word of God.

In giving the 10 Commandments, God prominently declared "you shall not commit adultery." This commandment is listed right after "thou shalt not kill." Every word of God is given by inspiration and is placed where it is for a reason. There is no such thing as "it didn't really matter to God what the order is." God had a very specific reason for putting the command not to commit adultery between thou shalt not kill and thou shalt not steal. This is because in a spiritual sense, committing adultery also breaks these other commandments. The wise King Solomon said the adulterer destroys his or her own soul. When you are committing adultery, you are stealing another person's husband or wife. This is why adultery has such dire consequences. The apostle Paul said, fornicators and adulterers God will judge (Hebrews 13:4).

God will hold adulterers accountable. Adultery is described as fulfilling an extremely wicked plan, and you are committing an outrageous crime. It is for this reason that adultery is an offense worthy of condemnation by God and man.

In the Old Testament, adultery was punishable by death. In the New Testament, while it is no longer a capital offense, God punishes it by putting a person in the furnace where all your good works are burnt up because you have made them of naught by committing adultery. This is not to suggest that there are no consequences in this life. When such immorality becomes accepted conduct in a family, it brings that family to destruction. Adulterers are covenant breakers. When a couple gets married, they enter into a covenant with God. The seductress is the one who forsakes the companion of her youth and forgets the covenant of God.

In 1 Corinthians 6:18, the Apostle Paul warns us to, "Flee fornication. Every sin that a man doeth is without the body; but he that committeth fornication sinneth against his own body."

Paul's statement is very plain and direct. It is also important for us to take heed to it because Paul was the apostle of the gentiles (Romans 11:3). This does not mean that the rest of scripture is less important, quite the opposite. The reason for Paul being the apostle to the gentiles is very important is because there are many people today, including theologians, who try to downplay the writings of Paul. Instead, they tell us the words of Jesus in the gospels are more important.

They forget that Jesus is the incarnate Word while the scriptures are the written word. It is worth noting that as the Word, anything Jesus spoke would have been considered "new" scripture if he wanted it to be so. Yet, when tempted by the devil, rather than create new scripture with his words, Jesus always quoted already existing scripture, giving it divine authority. Rather than saying Paul's writings are somehow "inferior" to Jesus' words in the gospels, as gentiles, if anything, we should pay special attention to what he says about a subject.

Paul says every sin, with the single exception of adultery is committed outside the body. What he is saying is that these sins have external consequences. For example, when you steal you hurt someone else. The same is true for other sins, including murder, dishonoring your parents, and bearing false witness. Yet, when it comes to adultery it literally is in a class all by itself. While there is no question it brings harm to others, Paul says adultery is a sin against your own body.

A person can make some level of justification for other sins. Proverbs 6:30 says, "Men do not despise a thief, if he steal to satisfy his soul when he is hungry." But adultery has no other purpose than to fulfill the lusts of the body. God has placed you in Christ, making you holy and blameless in his sight. Jesus has called you to a brand-new life. A life no longer marred by sin but baptized by grace. You will be able to identify the fog of your sin's deception, which will motivate you to think and live purely, which is the only way to prevent immorality tomorrow.

The consequences you will pay for grieving our Lord, who redeemed you, are severe. Rest assured, you will be chastised in various ways as you fall under your loving Father's discipline. Yet even apart from that, there are other consequences that have nothing to do with chastening, instead they are a part of God's natural law of sowing and reaping. Among the consequences of breaking this law are dragging your reputation into the mud, loss of reward, and condemnation from God.

One day you will see Jesus face to face and be forced to explain why you committed adultery, and you will not be able to offer any justification for it. Instead, you will live with the hurt you have done to your husband or your wife. Among the things it will cost you are the loss of your respect, loss of your kid's respect, and a loss of trust and credibility. This will result in bringing shame to your family as your name is discredited in church and the community. Sadly, this shame will often remain long after a person sincerely repents and changes their life for the better. David will forever be known for his sin with Bathsheba. The shame of adultery can endure for a lifetime, bringing an embarrassment to yourself while plaguing your mind with memories that harm future intimacy with your husband or your wife. Additionally, when a person engages willfully in a sin, it has the potential to remove inhibitions against other sins as well. When you are living a life out of fellowship with God, the Holy Spirit can be grieved to where he goes silent in areas of your life. This can result in affecting your ability to know what is right to do in other important areas, because you have a defiled conscience.

Adultery brings about the shame and hurt of your friends. Shame and hurt to those who work with you at the workplace. Shame to your church family. Shame to your friends, and especially those you have taught about Jesus and told them you are a Christian. Possibly keeping some of them from accepting Jesus, thus being lost for eternity. All because of your actions.

You are following in the footsteps of friends you know, whose immorality caused you to grieve and bring pain to innocent children around you who are collateral damage and get hit by your shrapnel. You are bringing great pleasure to the enemies of God and all that is good. Rather than live a life of godly laughter, you cause rejoicing by your blasphemous behavior by those whose disrespect God and the church. Your body is not your own, but for the Lord; and the Lord is for the body. Do you know that you were created for the Lord and your husband first of all? The divine standard for marriage is a lifelong commitment to you and your husband or your wife.

Trust is the foundation that a marriage rests upon. When it is betrayed, the will is broken, and the lack of trust can remain long after your spouse forgives you, because the painful experience will replay over and over in their mind. This will cause them to not want to let their guard down again, for fear that the adulterous act could happen again. Trusting despite getting hurt is bad enough, but this trust is difficult to retain when you have cheated. Their lack of trust is like padding to lessen the blow if cheating happens again.

How could you take such beauty away from a beloved husband you promised to cherish? Such pain is often indescribable. Your adultery not only affects the marriage, it victimizes your relationship with your spouse, children, friends, family and yourself.

Your husband may suffer from pain, embarrassment and the stigma that comes from the awareness that the adultery has become known by members of the church and is now the subject of community gossip. Such acts serve to lower the integrity of your whole family, who may suffer because of your adultery. Your children do not want their parents to suffer. At first you think your adultery is inconsequential, until you realize later when the newness of the illicit relationship wears off, that you had neither consideration for the feelings and health of the ones you love, nor did you consider your own best interests. Where's the trust between you?

While some truly understand the consequences of what they have done, sadly, many only express worldly sorrow for getting caught and having to face the consequences (2 Cor. 7:9-10). Because this is not godly repentance, they have a tendency to cast blame on the innocent husband in order to throw off their own guilt. If this is you, then rather than seek restoration, sometimes you fight to keep the other person's spouse from getting any information on your phone. You play the games of making the innocent spouse call. Whatever your husband has told you, you use it against him. You spent a great deal of time trying to convince your friends and family that your husband caused the problems. You are trying to paint a picture of him, but you know better than anyone that this fabricated picture can never be a masterpiece.

Your friends, family, acquaintances and others may not readily socialize with you because they are afraid you may have eyes on their husband, while others may choose to slight you. People will distrust you around their own husband because of your adulterous reputation.

Is it logical for you to think the bible says you shall not commit adultery for no good reason? Where is your credibility? Your behavior speaks to you. Your adultery and guilt is like a cancerous sore. It grows and gets worse as time passes. Soon it will occupy your mind, invading your thoughts when you are not wanted. It causes sorrow, regrets worry and shame. Your thoughts certainly do not add to the happiness of any relationship. You may think about returning your husband and rekindling your marriage, but your adultery is a threat to your husband's life.

You know you've been committing adultery for so long and you became involved before you attempted to rectify your mistake, so you have to endure the potential wrath of your once unsuspecting husband's angry reaction, which could result in a very nasty and costly divorce.

You think you can easily repair the damage to your marriage if your husband discovers your infidelities. You feel it is just a matter of getting your husband to forgive you, which he is commanded to do, so if he doesn't it means he is the one not right with God, you tell yourself. That could happen, but it may not always be that simple. The consequences of your adultery could be long-term, even irreparable to your marriage. Broken trust, divorce, low self-esteem, severe depression, dysfunctional family, the formation of character, severe violence and imprisonment. These are just some of the side-effects of adultery. Your adultery is never right in your marriage and excuses are not accepted. The consequences are devastating, especially for your husband and your children.

Chapter 7

Satan Attacks Marriages

The Bible says in first Peter 5:8-9, "Be sober, be vigilant; because your adversary the devil, as a roaring lion, walketh about, seeking whom he may devour: Whom resist stedfast in the faith, knowing that the same afflictions are accomplished in your brethren that are in the world."

You cannot help but wonder if sometimes Satan sits back and laughs at you after you commit adultery, for he knows how foolish you are. Marriage can be extremely messy. You can do dumb things in your marriage, you hurt your husband, you make false assumptions and then after your misconduct, you attempt to manipulate the situation by spinning events in your favor. You think less about serving and more about being served. Instead of following God's word or advice from your godly husband, you put your hope in your friends and family more than Jesus Christ.

The bible warns us that Satan prowls around like a lion, seeking to devour you. Knowing this, why would you be so foolish as to allow Satan to ruin your marriage. You do plenty of stupid things on your own to ruin your marriage, you don't need any help. You can be sure that when you are causing your marriage to self-destruct, Satan enjoys having a front row seat so he can watch your folly and foolishness. Because you live in the flesh and not in the spirit, you and your husband can be talking about something big or small; then at just the right moment, you are faced with a decision. It is at that moment that you hear a call to go and return home to your mom. It is at this point where you will pick your own way to follow. You can either satisfy your sinful life or chose to follow the lead of the Holy Spirit. You can go down the way of having a nasty fight or decide to honor your husband by admitting you were wrong. The choice is yours to make of your own free will.

If you're fighting, the last thing you want to do is to be intimate with your husband. Conflict is a barrier to intimacy in your marriage. One of God's purposes for sex is to foster unity in your marriage. Not having regular sex with your husband is allowing a barrier to come between you. No sex in your marriage means you're less unified.

When you are both out of sorts with each other, you are not respecting each other, and it makes you weary. Very weary, because you don't know how to stop your adultery. Yet you are tired of dealing with that nuclear war of sin in your life.

The most basic response to any difficulty in your life when things are becoming difficult in a marriage is for Satan to lead your mind to adultery. In marriage, selfishness and foolishness are among the biggest weapons Satan uses to attack your relationship. Maybe you live in the same house with your husband, but you live separate lives. This lack of unity and fellowship with each other allows Satan to play with your mind. He uses the old saying, "the grass is greener on the other side of the fence," to convince you that you can find fulfillment in a sexual relationship with someone else. Part of the reason the grass always looks greener is there is not any long-term commitment required.

After your adultery, you avoid one another rather than doing the hard things of dealing with the elephant in the room. Or maybe you hide behind work in order to avoid dealing with issues in your marriage, then you find yourself using it as a front to satisfy another man. In the heat of your love with him, you say things on the phone that you will come to regret. You have friends who call this stupid talk. Words come out of your mouth and the instant they leave, you wish you could pull them back inside, but you cannot.

You begin to flirt with a man at work by saying nice things that are innocent such as complimenting him on his appearance. In turn, he finds you attractive and finds ways to go out of his way to show you love, the physical kind that is. Can you believe it. Sadly, he does not ever demonstrate the same kind of love to his own wife at home that he expresses to you. Seeking acceptance, your blindness goes beyond what would be safe and careless boundaries. You love your job and you pour yourself into it, to the detriment of your family.

The man at your job is a married man and you know all about him. When overtime is offered you jump at the chance, rationalizing that your boss needs you at work, when in reality you want to meet with your lover every day. If you're honest, your work matters more than your family. You cherish your other man more than you do your husband and your kids.

Lying can destroy trust in your marriage. You are lying because you are trapped and don't want to have your sin exposed. You've been secretly having an extramarital affair. Of course, you are embarrassed at the thought of anyone finding out. This fear causes you to become emotionally and spiritually immature, and you call yourself a Christian. In other words, you are committing adultery with someone with poor character.

It is sad to see your foolishness. This is the typical battlefield that the devil puts you through. He is like a roaring lion, looking for someone to devour. The devil's strategy is to destroy you and your marriage. The intruders that Satan uses to destroy your marriage are: your friends, family, work, children, adultery, smart phone, Internet, television, addiction, sex, outside hobbies and interests, and more. In reality, most of these things are not all that bad, but they can be destructive for your marriage when they come between you and your love for your spouse.

They don't wait for an invitation to intrude into your marriage. They just show up unannounced all by themselves. If you want to prevent that from happening, you must become active and protect your marriage by allowing God to be the center of your life. When Jesus is the center of your life, you will be able to recognize the snares of the devil. Upon seeing these dangers, you will be able to put up well-balanced boundaries for your life. "A prudent man foreseeth the evil, and hideth himself: but the simple pass on, and are punished" (Proverbs 22:3).

You must guard your marriage with such a ferocity that no one can come between the two of you and separate you, including your family and friends. You must protect the core element of your marriage, the love between you and your husband. This is not free, and it will not happen by accident, it will cost you a lot. But your marriage will be stronger while you invest in it. Your marriage is designed by God to be an exclusive club. You and your husband are to live in an arrangement that provides a safe place for you and him. There is no room for a third person to receive an equal share in the marriage, because that can be easily disrupt the safety of your relationship. With another person present in your life, your love gets divided. A part of your heart for your husband is taken away from him, which is where it belongs, and is given to another person.

You may tell your best friend how happy you are with your husband, but out of a misunderstood submission, you fail to let your husband know your feelings. You make the children a confidant and they become closer to you than your husband. Such situations seldomly arise out of bad intentions, but nevertheless they serve to betray the trust between you and your husband in the union that God intended to develop in the marriage.

Because you let the door open for the devil to enter your life, your husband never has the opportunity to hear from you what you tell others about him, and therefore he is robbed of the blessing of being able to provide for your needs. God hates your deception and indirectness, because it is honesty and love that builds a marriage, not the recommendations of outsiders.

Of course, there is nothing wrong with having close family and friends in whom you can confide, but if it drives you away from your husband, you have certainly stepped over the line. Marital love requires a great deal of safety for true intimacy to grow, as it brings out the most vulnerable and fragile parts of your character. But in order to say yes to your marriage, you must be able to say no to other things. If you do not learn to say no to others, you eventually find out that you have been saying no to your marriage. Marriage involves more than keeping the love between you and your husband, and no one else. That means also forsaking your spouse and leaving behind your close friends and family. For example, there are certain benefits to being single. One of these is not having to live in a long-term commitment to someone else, and there is a certain level of freedom you have to do things that a married man does not. Likewise, there are benefits to being married such as the intimate portion and knowing you have a helpmeet, which is why God created women. But when you get married, you should not be spending as much time with your single friends or vice versa, because the temptation is to want to have the benefits of both lifestyles. This leads to disaster.

The Bible says in Genesis 2:24, "Therefore shall a man leave his father and his mother, and shall cleave unto his wife: and they shall be one flesh."

Sometimes you feel disheartened to find that you had to say no to so many things to maintain your marriage commitment. But if you don't make forsaking a part of your life, you always run the danger of adding the wrong things to your marriage and subtracting the good closeness of honesty from your spouse. When this happens, you have unlocked your front door and invited the intruder to come in and make a wreck out of your home.

You have to learn to avoid extremes and find the right way to balance things in your life. You need outside relationships and activities to get some of your needs met that your husband simply cannot fulfill. But at the same time, you have to make sure that these external influences do not intrude into your marriage and take a part of your heart away from your husband. Love always protects, always trusts, always hopes, always perseveres. Love never fails.

There is no fear in love, but perfect love drives out fear because fear has to do with punishment. The one who fears is not made perfect in love. If you are burdened by such fears, the chances are they will distance yourself emotionally from your husband. Your fear causes you to take a part of your heart away from your husband and devote it to someone else. But this will only bring temporary satisfaction. Your imperfections will be accompanied by increased grace, compassion, and forgiveness. The only solution to this problem is to take responsibility for your sins and begin to repent and reconnect to God.

"Be not deceived; God is not mocked: for whatsoever a man soweth, that shall he also reap." (Galatians 6:7) The one who sows to please his sinful nature from that nature will reap destruction.

Loving your husband is more important than what other people think of you. You have to become honest in your life. Satan uses you commit adultery, which causes you to hurt your spouse because he wants to destroy your soul. Satan draws you in with lies. Satan puts false thoughts in your head, telling you adultery is not so bad, you will be doing it just this once." Sin always gives you a short-term gain in return for long-term punishment.

"Know ye not that the unrighteous shall not inherit the kingdom of God? Be not deceived: neither fornicators, nor idolaters, nor adulterers, nor effeminate, nor abusers of themselves with mankind, Nor thieves, nor covetous, nor drunkards, nor revilers, nor extortioners, shall inherit the kingdom of God." (1 Corinthians 6:9-10)

Keep in mind, God's word offers a sharp warning to those engaging in unrepentant adultery. I encourage you to heed the warnings and be careful with sexual immoral strife, and instead seek to be honest and sexually pure. When you reject her husband, Jesus, said if you engage in unrepentant adultery, you will not receive heavenly rewards.

""Flee fornication. Every sin that a man doeth is without the body; but he that committeth fornication sinneth against his own body." (1 Corinthians 6:18)

Repentance means to change your mind. You have been tempted with sinful thoughts. This means you must turn to God to deliver you from temptation. Rebuke bad thoughts when they enter your mind, because the Scripture says we are to engage in "Casting down imaginations, and every high thing that exalteth itself against the knowledge of God, and bringing into captivity every thought to the obedience of Christ" (2 Corinthians 10:5).

God says adultery is sin and wickedness, and you should view it as such. When changing your thought patterns, you can begin to turn away from sin so when you have repented of adultery, you can then act to remove all unnecessary friends and family from your life. In Mark 9:43-44, Jesus says, "And if thy hand offend thee, cut it off: it is better for thee to enter into life maimed, than having two hands to go into hell, into the fire that never shall be quenched: Where their worm dieth not, and the fire is not quenched."

For you, this means throw away your phone or computer that you used to commit adultery. You should never place yourself in situations where you'll be texting another man or woman to whom you feel a strong attraction to. You would be wise to delete all contacts in your phone, including chat rooms, Facebook, WhatsApp, Twitter, Snapchat, and every other tool that Satan uses to destroy your life and your marriage. Never flirt with any person other than your husband. Always flirt with your husband to avoid temptation.

In fact, you should take any temptation you have to renew your love with your husband. Place your husband above friends and parents. You should seek to protect and cultivate the relationship with your husband.

"Confess your faults one to another, and pray one for another, that ye may be healed. The effectual fervent prayer of a righteous man availeth much." (James 5:16)

You should confess any and every sin that you commit against God and also confess your sin to others. It may be difficult, but God says you should confess your sins to others. Satan leads you to flirtation. You flirt like a butterfly from one man to another and make all men feel like you love them. You have to be careful because it can break your marriage. When you allow these things to continue, you become a selfish wife. You become strong-minded in making sure that you always come first. You want to build a cheerful loving home with your husband. You're obsessed with material things. You care about material things over your house. Faith and spiritual fulfillment are not yours.

No matter how much your husband provides you with the type of lifestyle that would make most of the world envious, you're never content and become an attention seeker. You seem to lose interest in everything easily and are always looking for the next thing to jump into, then you wonder why you have a hard time focusing on your marriage.

The devil will attack the things you love to do. You are somehow disrespectful and rude to your husband. Respect for one another is a very important thing with the person you will spend the rest of your life with, so it should not be taken lightly.

These are very typical lines Satan uses to entice the woman who is living with the guilt of adultery: "you have to be in submission to your husband," but this is seen as a weakness and not a godly strength, even though the headship is your divine husband. He is commanded to take primary responsibility for you and live like a Christlike servant, providing leadership, protection and provision in the home. If he does not do these things, God will punish him. All you have to do is be submissive. Rather than be a divisive wife, chose to live life where you affirm your husband's leadership, rather than turned onto the wrong path and doing things your way.

The bible has this to say about how wives are to act in the marriage.

"Wives, submit yourselves unto your own husbands, as unto the Lord. For the husband is the head of the wife, even as Christ is the head of the church: and he is the saviour of the body. Therefore as the church is subject unto Christ, so let the wives be to their own husbands in every thing." (Ephesians 5:22-24)

Notice this is not to be a blind submission, but you are to submit in the same way that Christians are to submit to their head, which is Jesus. This does not mean that the men get off scott-free. God has instructions for them regarding their role in the relationship as well.

"Husbands, love your wives, even as Christ also loved the church, and gave himself for it; That he might sanctify and cleanse it with the washing of water by the word, That he might present it to himself a glorious church, not having spot, or wrinkle, or any such thing; but that it should be holy and without blemish. **So ought men to love their wives as their own bodies. He that loveth his wife loveth himself.**" (Ephesians 5:25-28)

Men are told to love you in the same way Jesus loves us. He loved us enough to give his very life for us on the cross, and he promises to meet our needs. What is worth noting is God knows how hard it is for men to do this, so he explained to us how to do this when he said we are to "love their wives as their own bodies." In other words, we are to love them in the same way we would go out of the way to meet our own needs.

Satan's tactics are to drive a wedge between you and your husband by getting you to resist him and his God-given roles. When you do this, Satan gets a foothold in you, enabling him to divide your marriage and set you against your husband. Satan is working through you to destroy your own life. Satan uses you to attack your own marriage by committing nonstop adultery.

Marriage is a divine institution created by God, and now he wants to destroy it. Will you change your heart and your mind and turn to God to deliver yourself from your terrible and embarrassing sin? This enemy hates God and he hates marriage because marriage is portrayed as being of the Lord. Satan wants you to enter into a pattern of obeying desires instead of God's direction. God's ways are good, but Satan wants you to believe they are not. This is part of his diabolical plan ever since the garden of Eden. Don't let him succeed by causing adultery in your marriage.

Chapter 8

The Difference Between a Godly Wife and an Ungodly Wife

Who can find a virtuous woman? for her price is far above rubies. The heart of her husband doth safely trust in her, so that he shall have no need of spoil. She will do him good and not evil all the days of her life.

She seeketh wool, and flax, and worketh willingly with her hands. She is like the merchants' ships; she bringeth her food from afar. She riseth also while it is yet night, and giveth meat to her household, and a portion to her maidens. She considereth a field, and buyeth it: with the fruit of her hands she planteth a vineyard.

She girdeth her loins with strength, and strengtheneth her arms. She perceiveth that her merchandise is good: her candle goeth not out by night. She layeth her hands to the spindle, and her hands hold the distaff. She stretcheth out her hand to the poor; yea, she reacheth forth her hands to the needy.

She is not afraid of the snow for her household: for all her household are clothed with scarlet. She maketh herself coverings of tapestry; her clothing is silk and purple. Her husband is known in the gates, when he sitteth among the elders of the land.

She maketh fine linen, and selleth it; and delivereth girdles unto the merchant. Strength and honour are her clothing; and she shall rejoice in time to come. She openeth her mouth with wisdom; and in her tongue is the law of kindness.

She looketh well to the ways of her household, and eateth not the bread of idleness. Her children arise up, and call her blessed; her husband also, and he praiseth her.

Many daughters have done virtuously, but thou excellest them all. Favour is deceitful, and beauty is vain: but a woman that feareth the LORD, she shall be praised. Give her of the fruit of her hands; and let her own works praise her in the gates.

(Proverbs 31:10-31)

If you are a godly woman, you don't conform to popular fads. Your husband will have full confidence in your abilities and word. A godly woman has a strong interest in family values. She brings her husband no shame or harm, but the ungodly woman brings shame and harm to her husband all the time.

A godly woman works to help the family. She is a wise with your money. An ungodly woman doesn't know the value of money and spends it frivolously on herself. She hits all the sales and her closet is full of clothes she hasn't worn in years, and she has enough shoes to open her own store.

An ungodly woman doesn't build up her husband so that he is respected in the community. Because of her wrongdoing, she doesn't speak with wisdom. If you are a godly woman, you will live a life of faith and you will love the Lord.

An ungodly woman invests her money unwisely and buys everything she sees on TV. A godly woman invests money wisely, seeking good returns and then uses these investments to do good.

A good woman is a manager of her own affairs to ensure they prosper. Everything she does is to advance her relationship with Jesus. She loves God and is not forced to do right. God's word is her GPS by which she seeks to guide her life. But for the ungodly woman, you can rest assured that the devil guides her and seeks to ruin her life.

A good woman communes with God and has an intimate relationship with him. An ungodly woman prefers communing with friends rather than God. A godly woman is passionate about Jesus and her heart's desire is to share the word of God with others and she seeks to keep and obey his commandments. She seeks to please her husband and God above everything else. An ungodly woman doesn't please her husband and God. She puts herself and her friends above her husband and God.

A godly wife is deeply rooted in the Word of God. She knows that her achievements, love, career and family without Jesus are all in vain. Her main goal is to submit to her husband and raise her children in the nurture and admonition of the Lord. Jesus is respected by her husband, but more than anything she cares about him living for God and doing what God told him to do.

But the ungodly woman is selfish about her husband. She could care less about living the Proverbs 31 life. She doesn't understand that her husband can't fulfill her every need and desire, only Jesus can. She is not discrete. When she has problems with her husband, she always calls her parents, asking them to call the police on him. Because she doesn't know prayer changes things, she doesn't know that marriage is a picture of the relationship between Jesus Christ and church.

The ungodly woman will feed the acts of the flesh in her life. The actions of the flesh are obvious.

"Now the works of the flesh are manifest, which are these; Adultery, fornication, uncleanness, lasciviousness, Idolatry, witchcraft, hatred, variance, emulations, wrath, strife, seditions, heresies, Envyings, murders, drunkenness, revellings, and such like: of the which I tell you before, as I have also told you in time past, that they which do such things shall not inherit the kingdom of God." (Galatians 5:19-21)

For the godly woman, her love is not conditional. The ungodly wife is passionate about the temporal things of the world. She seeks to have the fruits of the Spirit.

"But the fruit of the Spirit is love, joy, peace, longsuffering, gentleness, goodness, faith, Meekness, temperance: against such there is no law." (Galatians 5:22-23)

If you want to be the wife God designed you to be, continue digging deep in the word of God, pray and be sensitive to the Holy Spirit's leading. Allow Jesus to sanctify you and change your life. Ask Jesus to change you so you can become a good wife who will be deeply blessed one day. Let go of adultery, friends, parents, phones, computer, TV shows or anything else taking your heart away from God.

A good wife may not have a lot of friends, but the friends she does have should be Christians or good moral people who keep her accountable and push her closer to Jesus. When she looks at her friends, they are a reflection of her. The bible says, "can two walk together except they be agreed" (Amos 3:3)

The godly wife is trustworthy and always has the best interests of those she loves on her heart. She is an asset and not a liability to her husband. Whatever good comes to her husband can be directly attributed to her.

The ungodly wife doesn't support and encourage her husband. She is unfaithful to him all of her life. She does not do her best to help her husband, instead she allows herself to be fooled by the devil because she will not listen to her husband.

You see, there is a way for her husband to be praised and cherished. But she is not a faithful wife who loves the Lord. Rather than remain faithful to her marriage vows she introduces a strange man into her marriage. She stays out and doesn't come home at a decent hour.

"Say unto wisdom, Thou art my sister; and call understanding thy kinswoman: That they may keep thee from the strange woman, from the stranger which flattereth with her words.

For at the window of my house I looked through my casement, And beheld among the simple ones, I discerned among the youths, a young man void of understanding, Passing through the street near her corner; and he went the way to her house,

In the twilight, in the evening, in the black and dark night: And, behold, there met him a woman with the attire of an harlot, and subtil of heart. (She is loud and stubborn; her feet abide not in her house: Now is she without, now in the streets, and lieth in wait at every corner.)

So she caught him, and kissed him, and with an impudent face said unto him, I have peace offerings with me; this day have I payed my vows. Therefore came I forth to meet thee, diligently to seek thy face, and I have found thee. I have decked my bed with coverings of tapestry, with carved works, with fine linen of Egypt. I have perfumed my bed with myrrh, aloes, and cinnamon.

Come, let us take our fill of love until the morning: let us solace ourselves with loves. For the goodman is not at home, he is gone a long journey: He hath taken a bag of money with him, and will come home at the day appointed.

With her much fair speech she caused him to yield, with the flattering of her lips she forced him. He goeth after her straightway, as an ox goeth to the slaughter, or as a fool to the correction of the stocks; Till a dart strike through his liver; as a bird hasteth to the snare, and knoweth not that it is for his life.

Hearken unto me now therefore, O ye children, and attend to the words of my mouth. Let not thine heart decline to her ways, go not astray in her paths. For she hath cast down many wounded: yea, many strong men have been slain by her. Her house is the way to hell, going down to the chambers of death." (Proverbs 7:4-27)

For the ungodly woman, her house is stressful and full of fighting and strife. Her ways will lead her husband to early death from all the worrying, heartache and pain. She speaks seductive and persuasive words in her phone to seduce men into immoral actions.

The reward for doing good is life, but sin leads only to more sin. If you are listening to your husband even when he corrects you, you will live. If you will not admit that you are wrong, you are in danger. If you are good, you are going to be honest. If you can't be trusted, you will be destroyed by your own dishonesty. The Lord protects honest people and destroys those who do wrong.

"A virtuous woman is a crown to her husband: but she that maketh ashamed is as rottenness in his bones." (Proverbs 12:4)

The reward depends on what you say and what you do. You will get what you deserve. If you repent of your sins you will live, but if you keep sinning you will die. Because there are two things God cannot do, even if he is a loving God. He cannot bring a sinner to heaven who has rejected what his Son did on Calvary, and he cannot lie. When you tell the truth, justice is done but lies lead to injustice. How good it is to get what you want, but if you refuse to turn away from adultery you will keep bad companions. Instead, the companions for the wise will cause you to become wise. If you make friends with sinners, you will be ruined.

Trouble follow sinners everywhere, but the righteous will be rewarded with good things. Be honest and have reverence for the Lord. Be dishonest and show that you don't. Your joy is your own, your bitterness is yours, no one can share them with you.

You are a foolish wife if you don't care about your sin, but a good wife wants to be forgiven and sin no more. Do yourself a favor and learn all you can, then remember what you learned, and you will prosper in your life. If you tell lies and commit adultery, you cannot escape the punishment. You are doomed. Keep God's laws and you will live long. If you ignore them you will die.

Obey God and you will live a long life, one filled with contentment and safe from harm. If you listen to advice and are willing to learn from your failure, one day you will be a better person and you will learn when you are correct. Only a disgraceful wife or husband commits adultery. You may think everything you do is right but remember that the Lord judges your motives.

You cannot lie and hide anything from God. You can lie to people, but you cannot lie to God. Don't be envious of sinful people. Let reverence for the Lord be the concern of your life. He knows your heart and what you are thinking. Selfishness only causes trouble. You're much better off to trust the Lord. Evil people are trapped in their own sins, honest people are happy and free.

If you are telling the truth you will be free and happy, but if you are telling lies you will be in bondage and unhappy. Ask God to let you have two things before you die. To keep you from lying and keep you from hell. Neither be an unfaithful wife or husband. If you have been foolish enough to be a disrespectful wife, stop and think of how hard it is to find a good wife. She is worth far more than jewels.

Her husband puts his confidence in her and he will never be poor. So long as she lives she does him good and never harm. She is strong and respected and not afraid of the future.

But the immoral wife will bring shame to her husband. She dresses inappropriately, showing her body to the world. She will put her job and pleasure above her husband. She only cares about her kids dressing nice. She's not concerned with her spiritual life. She will give out her phone number, and flirt with a man who she finds attractive just to have a good time. She does anything that makes her happy, whether it is right of wrong.

An adulterer screeches at the word submission and will not submit to her husband. She is very quarrelsome, and when she is having problems with her husband, she will call her parents and friends to drag him down. She will say to her husband, I love you, but she keeps committing adultery. She does not have a relationship with God, so she expects her husband to fulfill her desires.

The pain of adultery can make you sad or you can live a life of purity and be happy. It is your choice. Jesus can restore you if you are willing to admit that you are wrong. True repentance is unconditional and takes full responsibility for your wrongdoing. If you are truly repentant, you will be desperate to be forgiven and focus on what you have done rather than placing blame or responsibility on your husband who was faithful to you.

Sexual sin hardens the heart and closes off forgiveness. When you are caught in sin you are in the darkness and you cannot see the things you stumble over. Because of pride and disobedience, you are often more concerned about the feelings of your boyfriend over the feelings of your husband. Every night you send explicit text messages to your boyfriend to make him happy, while your husband waits in the bed by himself alone. Your actions reveal the condition of your heart.

There are consequences for your sin, but there is hope if you repent and come to Jesus. Which way will you go? If you pay attention when you are corrected, you are wise. But if you refuse to learn, you're hurting yourself. If you accept correction you will become wiser. Pay attention to what you do and watch where you are going. It may save your life. You walk in darkness, stumbling and unable to see what you stumble over. Sexual sin describes a sense of confusion and a disconnect from the Lord. God can help your selfish heart if you change your mind and turn to him. Often you blame your husband for not being good enough, but you never check yourself to see the shame you bring to him by failing him.

For this reason, God gave you up to dishonorable passions to where you exchanged natural relations for that which are contrary to nature, and you likewise gave up relations with your husband and are consumed with passions for other men and are committing shameless acts with other men and receiving in yourself the dire penalty for your sin.

Chapter 9

Spiritual Adultery

Throughout the previous chapters we have dealt with the issue of physical adultery. As we have shown, adultery is a very serious thing in the eyes of God. Whenever a book tackles subjects like this, there are always those who will read it with a spirit of self-righteousness. They will rightly say, "I have never even thought about committing adultery against my spouse." If they are single, they can honestly say they are still keeping themselves pure until marriage. All of these things are to be commended, and it should be the norm for every Christian. However, just as Job had a case of self-righteousness when he was going through his trials when he said, "My righteousness I hold fast, and will not let it go: my heart shall not reproach me so long as I live," (Job 27:6), I would be remiss if I did not touch on another form of adultery that is arguably more severe than physical adultery.

In Ezekiel 16, God describes the nation of Israel by comparing it to a woman, going back to when she was a newborn and helpless. He talks about how he took care of her and provided for not just her needs, but many of her wants. Then he describes how despite all of this, she stepped out on him and committed spiritual adultery with false gods.

"But thou didst trust in thine own beauty, and playedst the harlot because of thy renown, and pouredst out thy fornications on every one that passed by; his it was." (Ezekiel 16:15)

"Thou hast also committed fornication with the Egyptians thy neighbours, great of flesh; and hast increased thy whoredoms, to provoke me to anger." (Ezekiel 16:26)

"Thou hast played the whore also with the Assyrians, because thou wast unsatiable; yea, thou hast played the harlot with them, and yet couldest not be satisfied. Thou hast moreover multiplied thy fornication in the land of Canaan unto Chaldea; and yet thou wast not satisfied herewith. How weak is thine heart, saith the Lord GOD, seeing thou doest all these things, the work of an imperious whorish woman; In that thou buildest thine eminent place in the head of every way, and makest thine high place in every street; and hast not been as an harlot, in that thou scornest hire; But as a wife that committeth adultery, which taketh strangers instead of her husband!" (Ezekiel 16:28-32)

Additionally, God uses this same analogy in the book of Hosea where he commands the prophet Hosea to marry a woman who is a known adulterer to drive home what Israel has done to him.

"The beginning of the word of the LORD by Hosea. And the LORD said to Hosea, Go, take unto thee a wife of whoredoms and children of whoredoms: for the land hath committed great whoredom, departing from the LORD." (Hosea 1:2)

In the New Testament, those who have put their faith in Jesus and his finished work at Calvary to save them, realizing they can do nothing to earn their salvation, are called members of the "bride of Christ." The bible says that while we are individuals, we compose the body that makes up this bride. I am not going into great theological details about this because that is not the purpose of this book. Rather, my purpose is simply to show that Christians, male and female, are referred to as his bride.

Just as there are expectations for how a husband and wife are supposed to interact in a relationship, God has the same expectations for us as his bride. We have seen that the bible condemns adultery on multiple occasions, so if this is obviously a sin that God despises, how much more so if we as believers commit spiritual adultery against his Son.

If you are a Christian who is faithful to your wife or husband, I praise God for that and commend you. However, how faithful are you, as the bride, to your future husband, Jesus Christ?

While it is true that works plays no part in salvation, this does not mean that God has no expectations of us. Ephesians 2:8-9 are some of the most well-known verses that show we are saved by grace through faith, not of works.

"For by grace are ye saved through faith; and that not of yourselves: it is the gift of God: Not of works, lest any man should boast." (Ephesians 2:8-9)

While these verses are excellent for leading a person to Christ, we must never forget that after the ninth verse there is a verse ten.

"For we are his workmanship, created in Christ Jesus unto good works, which God hath before ordained that we should walk in them." (Ephesians 2:10)

God intends for us to walk in good works, not to get saved, but because we are saved. Moreover, going back to the marriage relationship, the bible says he wants his bride to be pure.

"Husbands, love your wives, even as Christ also loved the church, and gave himself for it; **That he might sanctify and cleanse it with the washing of water by the word, That he might present it to himself a glorious church, not having spot, or wrinkle, or any such thing; but that it should be holy and without blemish.**" (Ephesians 5:25-27)

Let me ask you a question, are you living a life without spot or wrinkle? I am not talking about perfection, I am referring to your personal walk with the Lord and are you living a life that is holy?

David said, "I will put no wicked thing before mine eyes." What are your eyes seeing? Are they watching television shows that feature women who are scantily-clad? Notice I did not say naked, for I hope the answer to that would be no. However, Jesus said that if you look on a man or woman with lust in your heart you are committing adultery. You cannot possibly tell me that you can watch most of the television shows and even the commercials today with the way women dress and tell me when you see them you are thinking about Amazing Grace.

I could also go on to talk about other issues, such as sports and other hobbies. When your favorite sports team plays during church time, do you stay home to watch the game? I will go even further. If you normally arrive at church 15 minutes early, then on the days when your team is playing, while you may still attend the service, do you stay in the parking lot until the last minute, listening to the game on the radio? If you do these things, then you are committing spiritual adultery for you are giving your affections to something else other than God.

What about some of the nice things you have? There is nothing wrong with things such as a nice car, boat, a nice house, furniture etc. However, how is your tithe? Do you find yourself fighting to make the tithe because of the debt you are in over your things? For that matter, suppose you can say that you always pay the tithe. Great, but if pastor says they are taking up a special offering for a missionary, do you have to let the plate go by because you do not have extra money. You pay the tithe, which is great but if you are spending all the rest of your money on things, you are committing spiritual adultery.

How about your television and reading habits? How much time do you spend watching TV or reading a newspaper or book each night? Now compare that to how much time you spend in your bible. I would like you to hold up a regular piece of paper. Do you realize if you would read enough bible each day to fill up two pieces of paper both front and back, you could read your entire bible in a year?

So, do you read your bible through in a year? If not, when you view it that way, that is pathetic. How can you say you love God, when you won't even take time to read two pieces of paper each day from the only book God ever wrote? For that matter, reading your bible through once a year really isn't that big of an accomplishment. If you were to time yourself, you would probably find reading the equivalent of those two pieces of paper is a tiny fraction of the time you spend in the bible. Yet, we make it sound so wonderful if a Christian reads through his entire bible once a year.

Do you realize that before the printing press, people would gather in church services where a person would just get up and read the bible for hours on end. When the speaker would get tired, the crowd would shout like fans at a football game, "keep reading," until he or someone else got back up there.

Do you brag on your groom, Jesus, to the world, telling everyone how excited you are to be his bride? Do you tell people when he gives you some new gift or blessing, or do you just keep these things to yourself, or if you do tell people, is it only in a church setting where it is "safe?" If you do these things, I don't care how faithful you are to your spouse, you are a spiritual adulterer and you are just as wicked as a man or woman who steps out on their spouse.

I am not saying these things to be harsh or condemning. I am speaking them in the spirit of love. There is coming a day when Jesus will return for his bride. When that day comes we will receive rewards for how we have served him down here on earth. I don't want you to have nothing at his coming. I am pleading with you to remain faithful to your groom and live a life of holiness.

In closing, I would like to leave you with a couple of final thoughts on how much Jesus loves you and why you should seek to remain pure for him and not commit adultery, spiritual or otherwise.

In order to help our limited minds grasp the greatness of God's love compared to how limited our ability to love is, God created on eternity's morning an example in the heaven's to illustrate this.

Down here on earth, one of the greatest symbol of love that transcends all borders and cultures is a red rose. Each Valentine's Day and Mothers Day, countless roses are purchased and given as a symbol of love. They are displayed at weddings and given anytime a person wants to express how much they love someone.

Yet if you look at this beautiful flower, you will discover it has thorns. This is a picture of the fact that although we are a "new creature" in Christ, we still have an old nature that seeks to do evil and thinks only of self. No matter how hard we try, our love can never be perfect, whether that love be directed to others or God, just like every rose has thorns.

However, there is one rose that is perfect. You won't find it here on earth, but if you look up at night, it is there in the heavens. In a region of our Milky Way galaxy in which we live, near the end of a giant molecular cloud in the Monoceros region, if you look up there, some 5,000 light years away from earth you will see a beautiful red object.

This object is known as the Rosette Nebula. It is a giant gas cloud that looks like a beautiful red rose. However, there is a difference between this rose and our roses here on earth. This rose happens to be 1,300 light years across. To help you understand how great this distance is, a light year is the distance light travels in a single year. The speed of light is 186,000 miles PER SECOND. I'll let you do the math to figure out how many miles across this rose is. When we consider that in one light second you could travel around the world almost eight times, you begin to get an idea of the size of this object.

This object was created back in the beginning in Genesis 1, yet it wasn't discovered until the mid-1800s with the advent of the telescope by Sir William Herschel. When he saw it for the first time, it had been there waiting to be discovered. This is a perfect picture of 1 John 4:19, "We love him, because he first loved us."

While we live down here on earth, we lift up our earthly rose, a symbol of love, to our God while exclaiming, "I love you Jesus." As we do so, it makes our heart glad for we are expressing our words with the greatest symbol of love human beings down here on earth have used for centuries.

Up in the heavens, God reaches down and accepts our love, giving us a beaming smile to show us he has accepted our token of love, indicating we are "accepted in the beloved" (Ephesians 1:6).

Then, he responds by saying, "I love you too," as he presents his rose to us. The greatest rose is the Rose of Sharon, a picture of Jesus (Song of Solomon 2:1) in the greatest book on love in the bible. But since we don't have any pictures of Jesus to remember him by, God shows us a heavenly image of the Rose of Sharon. The Rosette is there in the heavens, and unlike our earthly roses that contain thorns and will quickly wither and die, just like our lives which are but a vapor; His rose is steadfast in the heavens, a symbol of his eternal love.

When we bask in his love, it is such a beautiful feeling. However, when we compare it to our beautiful rose that we presented to him, suddenly we realize how seemingly insignificant our love is compared to his majestic symbol of love in the heavens. It is then when we realize how much God's heart swells at this comparatively miniscule amount of love to His, that we begin to appreciate even more that he would love unworthy sinners like us.

My friends, how much more does Jesus have to do to show us his great love. What more will it take for you to decide he is worth all you have to offer. Not because you need to do this for salvation, but just to reciprocate his great love.

Whenever we talk about heaven, it is always in the context of a wonderful place. The bible offers a partial description in the final chapters of Revelation and it is beautiful. It is a place where there is no sickness, pain or death. Never again will parents have to bury a child. We will never know what it means for someone we love to die of cancer or in a traffic accident. There is no crime, no murders, no robberies, no lying politicians, everything is perfect. If that were not enough our own bodies are perfect in every way. There is no such thing as being overweight. No one is missing a limb or has any disease that makes their lives miserable. It cannot be any better than this. Does this make you excited?

But wait a minute! Look over there! Something doesn't seem quite right. I don't know what it is, since everything is perfect, but there's someone who doesn't seem quite right compared to the rest of us. Let's go and check him out.

As we get closer, we see our observations were correct. Here is a person whose body isn't perfect like ours. They have open wounds in their hands, feet and sides. How can this be? Suddenly it dawns on us, this is Jesus. The bible says when John saw Jesus he was "as a lamb that had been slain." In other words, you could look and see this person had suffered a violent death.

For all eternity, we will have a perfect body and live in a perfect place. Yet in the midst of all this, there is one person who will never have a perfect body. This person is Jesus, the only person who never sinned.

But he will forever bear the wounds that he sustained from becoming sin for us and paying our price for all eternity. I don't know how you feel about that, but this doesn't seem fair to me.

I want to weep when I think that the only imperfect thing in heaven is Jesus. Why is this? God wants to make sure that when ten million years have passed and eternity is just beginning, we never forget the horrible cost of our redemption, so we could be there.

After all this, let me ask you, how can you refuse to serve him now? If this doesn't make you love him so much that you will do anything for him, then you are the most ungrateful person in the world and I don't know what else to say.

Please, do not commit adultery.

Printed in the United States
By Bookmasters